D1196931

Dramatic Irony in Chaucer

# Dramatic Irony in Chaucer

By

GERMAINE DEMPSTER, Ph.D.

THE HUMANITIES PRESS

New York 1959

First Published in 1932 by Stanford University Press

Reprinted 1959 by The Humanities Press
by special arrangement with
Stanford University Press
and the author

PRINTED IN THE U.S.A.
by Noble Offset Printers, Inc.
New York 3, New York

# PREFACE

The scope of the present study is somewhat wider than its title may at first suggest. An analysis of any writer's treatment of dramatic irony would necessarily involve the plots chosen, the mood pervading the stories, and many features of narrative technique. But Chaucer's particular case calls for even further considerations. Let the reader call to mind the most striking cases of dramatic irony in our poet's works and he will observe that some occur in passages almost literally translated from well-known sources, while others are found in what are generally regarded as Chaucer's most original pieces of work. This suggests a study of the sources in the hope of finding influences under which Chaucer first came to make use of the device, factors in his growing taste for it, and—most interesting of all—the quality and extent of what seem to be his own creations. I have accordingly given much space not only to comparisons with extant originals but also to discussions of hypothetical sources, thus venturing into dangerous and consequently most enticing fields.

Having thoroughly enjoyed the research done in preparation for this book, I experience a new and very real pleasure in expressing my deep gratitude, first of all, to the C.R.B. (Commission for Relief in Belgium) Educational Foundation, to which, after the completion of my studies at the University of Liège, I owe the great privilege of two years at Stanford University, where the present work was undertaken.

My indebtedness to Professor J. S. P. Tatlock, then of Stanford University, can hardly be measured. To him I owe my initiation into medieval literature, an initiation that determined my enthusiastic choice of this field. During my stay at Stanford University, Dr. Tatlock suggested to me the subject of this study, and the work developed under his ever kind and inspiring guidance. After my departure he has followed its further development even to the point of publication.

It is also a pleasure to record here my obligations to several members of the faculty of the University of Chicago. I am especially thankful to Professor James R. Hulbert for directing my attention to an early text I had overlooked, and to Professor Walter L. Bullock for kindly helping me through some difficult passages in Italian.

G. D.

CHICAGO, ILLINOIS
June 1932

# CONTENTS


PAGE

List of Abbreviations . . . 6

I. Introduction . . . 7

II. "Troilus and Criseyde" . . . 10
- Dramatic Irony and Determinism . . . 10
- Instances of Dramatic Irony in the Poem . . . 13
- Conclusions . . . 26

III. Chaucer's Fabliaux . . . 27
- The "Reeve's Tale" . . . 27
- The "Miller's Tale" . . . 35
- The "Shipman's Tale" . . . 39
- The "Friar's Tale" . . . 42
- The "Summoner's Tale" . . . 45
- The "Merchant's Tale" . . . 46

IV. The "Wife of Bath's Tale" . . . 59

V. The "Franklin's Tale" . . . 62

VI. The "Nun's Priest's Tale" . . . 68

VII. The "Pardoner's Tale" . . . 72

VIII. The Frame of the "Canterbury Tales" . . . 80

IX. Narratives with Little or No Dramatic Irony . . . 83
- The "Legend of Good Women" and the "Manciple's Tale" . 83
- The "Monk's Tale" . . . 86
- The "Canon's Yeoman's Tale" . . . 87
- The "Knight's Tale" . . . 87
- The "Clerk's Tale" . . . 91
- The Three Pious Legends . . . 91

X. Conclusions . . . 94

Index . . . 99

# LIST OF ABBREVIATIONS

| | |
|---|---|
| *Angl.* | *Anglia* |
| *Angl. Beibl.* | *Anglia-Beiblatt* |
| *Archiv.* | *Archiv für das Studium der Neueren Sprachen* |
| Ch. Soc. | Chaucer Society |
| *Cl. T.* | *Clerk's Tale* |
| *C.T.* | *Canterbury Tales* |
| *C.Y.T.* | *Canon's Yeoman's Tale* |
| *Decam.* | *Decameron* |
| *Engl. Stud.* | *Englische Studien* |
| *Fil.* | *Il Filostrato* |
| *Fkl. T.* | *Franklin's Tale* |
| *Fr. T.* | *Friar's Tale* |
| *J.E.G.P.* | *Journal of English and Germanic Philology* |
| *Kn. T.* | *Knight's Tale* |
| *Legend* | *Legend of Good Women* |
| *Mch. T.* | *Merchant's Tale* |
| *Mcp. T.* | *Manciple's Tale* |
| *Mil. T.* | *Miller's Tale* |
| *Mk. T.* | *Monk's Tale* |
| *Mod. Lang. Notes* | *Modern Language Notes* |
| *Mod. Lang. Quar.* | *Modern Language Quarterly* |
| *Mod. Lang. Rev.* | *Modern Language Review* |
| *Mod. Phil.* | *Modern Philology* |
| *M.L.T.* | *Man of Law's Tale* |
| *N.P.T.* | *Nun's Priest's Tale* |
| *Or. and An.* | *Originals and Analogues of the "Canterbury Tales"* (Ch. Soc.) |
| *Pd. T.* | *Pardoner's Tale* |
| *P.M.L.A.* | *Publications of Modern Language Association of America* |
| *Pr. T.* | *Prioress' Tale* |
| *Rom.* | *Romania* |
| *Rv. T.* | *Reeve's Tale* |
| *Sh. T.* | *Shipman's Tale* |
| *S.N.T.* | *Second Nun's Tale* |
| *Spec.* | *Speculum* |
| *Sum. T.* | *Summoner's Tale* |
| *Tes.* | *Teseide* |
| *Tr. and Cr.*, or *Troilus* | *Troilus and Criseyde* |
| *W.B.P.* | *Wife of Bath's Prologue* |
| *W.B.T.* | *Wife of Bath's Tale* |

# DRAMATIC IRONY IN CHAUCER

## I. INTRODUCTION

Dramatic irony is the irony resulting from a strong contrast, unperceived by a character in a story, between the surface meaning of his words or deeds and something else happening in the same story. When Wallenstein, a few moments before being murdered, gives directions that he shall not be disturbed in his sleep,

> Ich denke einen langen Schlaf zu thun,
> Denn dieser letzten Tage Qual war gross,
> Sorgt dass sie nicht zu zeitig mich erwecken,[1]

the contrast between the surface meaning of his words and what the reader knows to be afoot constitutes dramatic irony. The condition essential to the existence of such irony—the fact that the character must be unconscious of the incongruity—rules out of our consideration the larger portion of contrasts involved in words or deeds. For those contrasts are often consciously created by a character—as when the innkeeper confers upon Don Quijote[2] the order of knighthood—or, in other cases, startling incongruities involved in human actions (and possibly felt as the workings of fate)[3] are as clearly perceived by the characters themselves as by the readers—as when Rodrigue kills the father of his beloved Chimène.[4]

Like any definition in matters of art, our definition of dramatic irony necessarily involves a subjective element, which, however, we may hope partly to eliminate by stating what kind of contrasts we consider strong enough to create dramatic irony. In any story there always is, if not for the reader, at least for one character, an element of unexpectedness that gives rise to certain incongruities between efforts, expectations, etc., on the one hand, and reality on the other hand. Those incongruities, however, cannot create dramatic irony unless at least one of two conditions is realized: either the words and deeds that constitute one element of the contrast

[1] *Wallenstein's Tod,* V, v.

[2] *Don Quijote,* Part I, chapter iii.

[3] I shall use the two phrases "dramatic irony" and "irony of action" as synonymous, referring to cases of irony that answer our definition. To the phrases "irony of fate" and "irony of circumstances," I give a wider meaning, applying them to irony involved not necessarily in our words or actions, but more generally in the circumstances of our lives, and without any implication either of perception or lack of perception of ironical contrasts on the part of the characters.

[4] *Le Cid,* I, vii.

must be something more than the natural and adequate reaction of a character to the situation as it appears to him, or the element of surprise, of the unforeseeable, must be absolutely startling in the real situation. The first condition is realized in the course of the scene where Lady Capulet attributes her daughter's tears to the death of her cousin Tybalt.[5] Her mistake, so far, is too natural for any contrast with the real facts to strike us as specially unexpected, but dramatic irony flashes up with her further interpretation of Juliet's grief as due to the fact that Tybalt's murderer, Romeo, is alive, an interpretation so false, and yet so true, that we are startled with wonder at the fate that must be planning such ironies. For the second of our two conditions, the adventures of Landolfo Ruffolo offer a good illustration:[6] Landolfo has been shipwrecked and keeps pushing back the floating chest that threatens to upset the plank on which he is left afloat, a perfectly natural action, which, however, creates dramatic irony because the said chest happens to contain the jewels that will ultimately save Landolfo from misery.

For the effectiveness or even the existence of dramatic irony there are other more intangible but equally important requirements. First, the interest of the reader in the characters: chance mocking jealous Simkin is so much more interesting and so much surer to be noticed than the similar chance that mocks his prototype in the French fabliau. And, secondly, the interest of the characters themselves in the part they enact: when the apothecary of the *Pardoner's Tale* assures his customer that he will be rid of all his rats, no irony comes out of the very real contrast thus created, because the apothecary, as far as we know, cares little or nothing whether his drug is used on vermin or on men.

Within the limits set by these requirements we find a whole range of cases varying from contrasts resulting from mere revulsion of feelings on the part of a character, or simple disappointment, or use of ambiguous words—rather weak cases, as a rule—to the violent and deeply tragic incongruities in the world of Thomas Hardy's novels. Irony may be derived from a logical opposition of one thing which is foreseen and the reverse which happens, but also from more elusive and subtle connections between elements that jar, though we cannot see exactly how or why. The power behind the curtain may have the definiteness of Greek ἀνάγκη, Mohammedan foreordination, or Christian Providence (the reader in each case accepting the philosophic background of the author), or the same power may be shrouded in perhaps more impressive mystery. Our feelings, in some cases, are hatred and rebellion against tyrannical powers; in other cases, reverent wonder, possibly combined with the intellectual pleasure of

[5] *Romeo and Juliet,* III, v.

[6] *Decam.,* II, 4.

questioning; in others still, genial optimism in a reconciliation with a friendly, soothing universe. The reader's moral instincts may be offered a pleasant gratification—or just the opposite, for dramatic irony and poetic justice cover different grounds;[7] there may be humor, or satire, or pathos, or any combination of all these moods.

Chapters ii to viii will be devoted to those narratives in which dramatic irony is a prominent feature. No attempt will be made to note all the cases of dramatic irony in such works, as enough material will be supplied by strokes which are of decided interest either for their beauty and significance within the narrative, their peculiarly Chaucerian character, or for the light they throw on the nature and extent of Chaucer's indebtedness to some of his masters in the use of the device. For attention will continually be given to the sources—known or hypothetical—in an attempt to weigh the different literary influences that helped our poet in developing both his taste for dramatic irony and his skill in handling it. In chapter ix we shall very briefly treat the narratives in which Chaucer, to a large extent, refrains from laying stress on the irony of action, in spite of opportunities often obvious enough. Superfluous as such a survey may seem at first sight, I feel that it is indispensable to our full appreciation of Chaucer's moderation in the use of the device, of his sure perception of all its nuances, as illustrated in the larger portion of our study.

Four narrative works of Chaucer will be omitted entirely: *Melibeus,* and the unfinished *Cook's Tale, Squire's Tale,* and *Tale of Sir Thopas,* none of which contains enough action for even the absence of dramatic irony to be of any interest. The *Physician's Tale* will be dismissed in a footnote to the three pious legends, and *Anelida and Arcite* in a footnote to the *Legend of Good Women.* All other narratives will be treated in the text, though the early allegories will be only briefly mentioned in connection with *Troilus and Criseyde.* Everywhere, familiarity with Chaucer's plots on the part of the reader is assumed.

---

[7] They often coincide because the reversal of fortunes that crowns many a "moral" story is an opportunity for dramatic irony. But dramatic irony may have nothing to do with merit or demerit, and may even derive some of its impressiveness from a reversal of moral values.

## II. *TROILUS AND CRISEYDE*

### Dramatic Irony and Determinism

The philosophical background of Chaucer's *Troilus and Criseyde* is fatalism of a somewhat confused character: Fortune sometimes appears as the fickle goddess so familiar in medieval literature,[1] sometimes as executrix of God's Providence, as in Boethius and Dante;[2] her powers, those of the bond of love and those of the stars (or of the pagan gods by the same names), somewhat overlap;[3] and the prayers of Troilus half imply that Destiny might yield to supplication. But we are not concerned here with the exact nuance of the determinism in the tragedy. We must confine ourselves to the bearing of the philosophical background on the effectiveness of dramatic irony, and all we need remember in that connection is the feeling of inescapable necessity with which the narrative proceeds. The whole tragedy is felt, not so much as a series of events occurring one by one in the course of time, but as one solid mass, as the reflection in this world of elements somehow inseparably woven together in another world. No atmosphere could be more favorable to the development of a keen sense of dramatic irony, both in the poet and in us, readers; conscious of the agency of something very different from mere chance, we shall suspect connections between motifs and episodes not clearly related by our stiff law of cause and effect, and shall miss none of the otherwise perhaps insignificant ironies of circumstance.

For the first suggestion of a fatalistic background to the tragedy of *Troilus,* Chaucer is evidently indebted to *Il Filostrato.* To be sure, our poet had long been familiar with the goddess Fortuna of medieval poetry—we remember the *Book of the Duchess*—and Boccaccio's hurried remarks about Destiny are often little more than conventional phraseology. Still, through their frequency, they do build up a certain decorative fatalism which it was easier and more natural for any translator or imitator to adopt than to reject. Also Chaucer's appreciation of the individual strokes

---

[1] Howard R. Patch, *The Goddess Fortuna in Mediaeval Literature* (Cambridge, 1927), and "Chaucer and Lady Fortune," *Mod. Lang. Rev.,* XXII (1927), 377–88.

[2] Howard R. Patch, *The Goddess Fortuna in the "Divine Comedy,"* Thirty-third Annual Report of the Dante Society (Boston, 1916), and "Troilus on Determinism," *Spec.,* VI (1931), 225–43; Bernard L. Jefferson, *Chaucer and the "Consolation of Philosophy" of Boethius* (Princeton, 1917), especially pp. 47 ff.

[3] As in the *Kn.T.;* see Walter C. Curry, *Chaucer and the Mediaeval Sciences* (New York, 1926), pp. 149–63.

of dramatic irony in the *Filostrato*—an appreciation of which we shall find abundant proof—without any doubt must have encouraged him at least to maintain the best possible background for such ironies, viz., that of foreordination.

If the first suggestion came from the *Filostrato,* much of Chaucer's serious handling of the question of determinism is due to Boethius.[4] Whether the conclusions reached in the *Consolation of Philosophy*—of which conclusions there is no trace in the *Troilus*—had been reconciled with Chaucer's own creed or not, much of Boethius' argument had become part of his very thought and often must have caused him to stop and ponder where Boccaccio had lightly dropped a purely conventional phrase.

The whole scope of Chaucer's acquaintance with classical antiquity is a third factor which may have weighed in favor of a fatalistic background. This acquaintance, I feel, must have disposed our poet to welcome determinism partly for its own artistic value, for the nobility and dignity which it imparts to human lives, partly as a very desirable note of local color.[5]

Whatever the relative importance of these influences, Chaucer deliberately set to work with a purpose not only of maintaining but of intensifying the feeling of inescapable necessity found in the *Filostrato.* What methods did he use?

First, he used Boccaccio's own methods, but with new emphasis and consistence. Instead of rather hurriedly announcing the coming sorrows of Troilus after his separation from Criseyde, Chaucer gives us more definite details:

> . . . . the double sorwes . . . .
> Of Troilus in lovynge of Criseyde,
> And how that she forsook hym or she deyde.[6]

---

[4] On the interest of Chaucer in the problem of foreordination and free will, see C. Brown, *P.M.L.A.,* XIX (1904), 128–30; J. S. P. Tatlock, *Mod. Phil.,* III (1906), 370–72, and XIV (1916), 265; Kate O. Petersen, *On the Sources of the "Nonne Prestes Tale"* (Boston, 1898), p. 93, note; B. Jefferson, *op. cit.,* pp. 47 ff.; D. Fansler, *Chaucer and the "Roman de la Rose"* (New York, 1914), pp. 210 ff.; H. Patch, *The Goddess Fortuna in Mediaeval Literature,* "Chaucer and Lady Fortune," and "Troilus on Determinism."

[5] On Chaucer's effort to give *Tr. and Cr.* an antique coloring, see J. S. P. Tatlock, "The Epilog of Chaucer's *Troilus,*" *Mod. Phil.,* XVIII (1921), 640 ff.

[6] *Tr. and Cr.,* I, 54–56. (For Chaucer's *Tr. and Cr.* I shall refer to book and lines, using the edition of R. K. Root [Princeton, 1926]; for *Fil.,* to book and stanza, from the edition of N. E. Griffin and A. B. Myrick, who give us both the text and an excellent translation into English [*The "Filostrato" of Giovanni Boccaccio* (Philadelphia, 1929)]. For the rest of Chaucer's works, I shall use the edition of Skeat.)

As the narrative proceeds, other lights thus quickly thrown on the future help to keep up that feeling that the predicted catastrophe is inevitable.[7] Similarly, Boccaccio's somewhat hasty remarks on the unconstant character of Fortune, sometimes simply translated, are more frequently enlarged upon, either by mild and cautious remarks in the vein of the Italian poet, or by definite statements inspired by Boethius and Dante:

> But O, Fortune, executrice of wyerdes,
> O influences of thise hevenes hye,
> Soth is that, under god, ye ben oure hierdes.[8]

And, finally, the monotonous and not very impressive chiding of blind Fortune by the Italian Troilo develops into an emphatic rejection of the theory of free will.[9] This disquisition, along with the more Boccaccian passages that imply the hero's acceptance of foreordination as established truth, should of course be considered as distinct from the poet's own attitude, and yet, somewhat illogically, through their very length, they add considerable weight and body to the forces of Destiny behind the curtain.

A few other and more original additions to Chaucer's Italian model similarly contribute to intensify the feelings of fatalism: first, the much stronger connection established between the fate of the lovers and the

---

[7] E.g., *Tr. and Cr.,* IV, 8–18. Compare corresponding passages in *Fil.,* I, 3; III, 94. They are less effective because less definite. Boccaccio cannot make Criseida's betrayal the main issue, since his heroine, at least in the longer part of the poem, is more or less representing Maria d'Aquino, whose absence from Naples, the poet says, causes him as much grief as the absence of Criseida has inflicted upon Troilo. In this illustration, he tells us in his proem, lies the main point: *"l'altre cose, che oltre a queste vi sono assai, niuna, siccome già dissi, a me non appartiene, nè per me vi si pone, ma perchè la storia del nobile innamorato giovane lo richiede"* (Griffin and Myrick ed., p. 128). This is, indeed, dramatic irony in real life: those secondary *"altre cose"* constituted a startling prophecy of Boccaccio's own future sorrows when discarded by Maria.

[8] *Tr. and Cr.,* III, 617–19. Such statements, no doubt, were closer to Chaucer's own Catholic creed than were the conventional complaints against blind Fortune. But my feeling is that they are too few (besides the Epilogue, only III, 617 ff., just quoted, and V, 1541–45) to play the important part ascribed to them by H. Patch ("Troilus on Determinism," *Spec.,* VI [1931], 225–43), i.e., to give the real philosophical key in which the whole poem was written and should be read. If such is their significance, why so few? why none at all before we reach almost the middle of the third book? To most readers, the general impression will, I believe, always remain one of determinism distinctly more pagan than Christian. Personally I have little doubt that Chaucer's conception of art (like Boccaccio's) allowed him "to play with philosophy for the sake of a sensation" (Patch, *op. cit.,* p. 241).

[9] *Tr. and Cr.,* IV, 958–1078. Many other passages betray the hero's interest in the problem of predestination: I, 520, 568, 834–40; II, 526–28; III, 372–73, 1261–67, 1744–64; IV, 260–87.

Trojan war, itself previously associated in our memories—and probably in those of Chaucer's readers—with inexorable Destiny;[10] secondly, the extent and precision of the references to astrology, which, in the eyes of Chaucer's readers, must have given the fatalism of the tragedy both scientific support and half-familiar coloring. The distinction between lucky and unlucky days[11] produces an effect perhaps weaker but certainly related. Finally, creating out of the frivolous Italian Criseida our serious and gentle Criseyde, in love with "moral vertu grounded upon trouthe"[12] yet doomed to faithlessness, Chaucer has strengthened in us a conviction that the stars indeed, or Fortune, or whatever god there is, had planned the whole tragedy at the birth of the noble heroine.[13] This, however, may be only an accidental consequence of the delicate development of a character for its own sake. In the points previously mentioned—clear anticipations of the dénouement, numerous references to inevitable Fate, Troilus' soliloquy on free will, emphasis on the war background and on astrology—I believe that we see more clearly Chaucer's conscious and consistent building up, and keeping up, of a fatalistic atmosphere.

But does not this strongly emphasized fatalism deprive the ironies of life of their real impressiveness, the impressiveness of mystery? Paradoxical as it may seem, the background of the *Troilus* partakes of the advantages both of definiteness and of indefiniteness. Enough stress is laid on metaphysical considerations to enthrone Fortune as the power ruling over men, though, on the other hand, that power is not, so to speak, familiar enough to be accepted by the reader without a sense of mystery. Perhaps the secret of this lies in a unique compromise of classical conventions with Christian thought: a "Fortune" less whimsical than the traditional Fortune of Jean de Meung for instance, less cruel than the Greek Fate, executrix of God's will yet not quite of the Christian God's; the ruling power is an inescapable reality, and yet it has much of the majesty and impressiveness of the unknown.

## Instances of Dramatic Irony in the Poem

Rather than endeavor to note each of the many ironies of action in the *Troilus* we shall confine ourselves to the most interesting and character-

---

10 In Boccaccio, this war setting was reduced to its very minimum, which minimum, however, had to include the important opening of the first book, viz., the gods' revelations to Calchas.

11 Pandarus urges the suit of Troilus on May 3 (II, 56). On this question, see J. M. Manly, *Canterbury Tales* (New York, 1929), note to line 1850 of the *Kn. T.*, pp. 549 ff.

12 *Tr. and Cr.*, IV, 1672.

13 In this I do not agree with A. S. Cook's interpretation of Criseyde's character. See *P.M.L.A.*, XXII (1907), 531–47.

istic examples, grouping them in three sections: (1) instances of dramatic irony for which Chaucer is directly indebted to Boccaccio; (2) some which our poet grafted on situations supplied by the *Filostrato;* and (3) others found in episodes created by Chaucer.

1. *Dramatic irony supplied by or suggested in the "Filostrato."*—In order to form an opinion as to the part played by the *Filostrato* in the development of Chaucer's sense of dramatic irony, we must give much of our attention to episodes of secondary importance in the main plot. Of the ironical features which lie at the very core of the tragedy—the irony cast on the lovers' joys by the feeling that their happiness is to pass away so soon, and the similar irony of the hero's enthusiastic praise of the god of love, who is preparing his ruin—of these, Boccaccio, to be sure, had shown himself fully conscious, but he had pointed them out in rather conventional ways, never making them the center of his readers' interest. If Chaucer's stronger fatalism has thrown on these motifs the ironic light of great tragedy, the merit is largely his own.[14] But in the gusto with which dramatic irony is treated in the minor episodes of the *Filostrato* the Italian poet is at his best. His technique of presentation offers special interest for us. In his fear that we, unintelligent readers, may miss those delightful incongruities of life, Boccaccio stops to point them out to us in a clear but not entirely flattering way. For Chaucer much of this insistence was no doubt superfluous, for in the narrative poems written before *Troilus and Criseyde*[15] our poet had taken great pleasure in creating situations that involved misunderstandings or incongruities,[16] which was as big a step toward using dramatic irony as could be taken by a writer

[14] For this effect Chaucer does not rely on the background exclusively. He takes care, e.g., to interrupt the account of the lovers' happiness with this remark:

> And thus Fortune *a tyme* ledde in joie
> Criseyde and ek this kynges sone of Troie.
> —III, 1714–15

Boccaccio's similar remark (III, 94), occurring at the end of the account and by way of transition, fills a very different purpose.

For detailed comparisons of the English and Italian poems, see the notes in Root's edition of *Tr. and Cr.,* the tables of parallels of Rossetti (Ch. Soc., 1873), and H. M. Cummings, *The Indebtedness of Chaucer's Works to the Italian Works of Boccaccio* (1916), pp. 51 ff.

[15] That another poem of Boccaccio, the *Teseide,* should have been imitated by Chaucer before *Fil.* is only a possibility, which can be disregarded in the present study. On Chaucer and the *Tes.,* see chapter ix, pp. 87–91.

[16] E.g., the mourner of the *Book of the Duchess* mistaking for a naïve child the dreamer who is only simulating ignorance; or, in the *Hous of Fame,* the pedantic attitude of the eagle who expects to impress the poet with his learning while the latter's fears of being dropped leave no room for any other interest.

of allegories.[17] But an equally long step remained ahead, and it was a lucky accident which, at this juncture (i.e., quite early in the creative period of Chaucer's life), brought him to a close study of a poet who not only makes frequent and skilful use of dramatic irony but forces his readers to the clearest and most conscious form of responsive appreciation.

The parting visit of Criseyde's friends is a good example. In its liveliness and humor the scene strikes us as characteristic of Chaucer. The truth is that he contributed nothing to it. Exactly as in our *Troilus,* the Trojan ladies in the *Filostrato* discuss the pros and cons of the exchange of prisoners in the presence of poor Criseida, to whom Calchas and politics are equally uninteresting topics. One of the visitors shares in the pleasure that Criseida no doubt must feel at the prospect of seeing her father; another regrets that she should leave them so soon. Criseida hears it all, but her thoughts remain with Troilo. We feel pity for her, slight impatience with the intruders' *"parlar femminili,"* but above all we are amused at the misunderstandings on which the whole scene rests. All this before we reach the end of stanza 82. Yet Boccaccio proceeds:

> E queste donne che far le credeano
> Consolazione stando, sommamente
> Parlando seco assai le dispiaceano,
> Come a colei che sentia nella mente
> Tutt'altra passion che non vedeano
> Color che v'erano.[18]

Criseida cannot repress her tears, which the visitors interpret as an expression of her grief at parting from—them! They try to comfort her "of that which does not grieve her." Stated in this way (st. 84, and st. 85, ll. 1–2), the irony comes out clearly enough. But Boccaccio does not feel safe yet:

> Parole assai dicean di consolarla
> Per la partenza la qual far dovea
> Da loro, e non era altra che grattarla
> Nelle calcagne, ove'l capo prudea.[19]

No comparison of the *Filostrato* with the English text will be necessary here: Chaucer follows the Italian very closely, showing thereby both his enjoyment of the ironies presented by Boccaccio and his approval of a somewhat rhetorical method of securing the readers' adequate appreciation. Of both, however, a more convincing illustration is found in the opening scene of the feast of Palladion, for Chaucer here uses several means of

[17] For real action, i.e., action involving elements of unexpectedness, requires a more direct contact of reader and object than allegory can create.

[18] *Fil.,* IV, 83.

[19] *Ibid.,* st. 85, ll. 3–6.

enlarging upon the dramatic irony of the *Filostrato:* more numerous contrasts, and increased emphasis through colorful expression and longer direct comments.

Heart-free and consciously enjoying his freedom, Troilus, like his Italian prototype, is strolling idly about the temple, scoffing at Love and his devotees. Boccaccio comments:

> O cecità delle mondane menti,
> Come ne seguon sovente gli effetti
> Tutti contrarii a' nostri intendimenti!
> Troil va ora mordendo i difetti,
> E' solleciti amor dell' altre genti,
> Senza pensare in che il ciel s'affretti
> Di recar lui il quale amor trafisse
> Più ch' alcun altro, prior del tempio uscisse.[20]

Chaucer translates the beginning of this stanza, but his amusement at the incongruities created by the action and his frank delight in a little familiar harmless teasing of his hero soon cause him to leave this somewhat solemn tone—which in his narrative has a delicate tinge of the mock-heroic—and continue in his own picturesque and ever refreshing language:

> This Troilus is clomben on the staire,
> And litel weneth that he moot descenden; . . . .
>
> As proude Bayard gynneth for to skippe
> Out of the wey, so pryketh hym his corn,
> Til he a lassh have of the longe whippe.[21]

Boccaccio's comment was shorter, and yet the lightness of touch is Chaucer's, and, along with that lightness, the vividness that stamps in our memories the amusing downfall of Troilus.

Other touches of dramatic irony are added to the same Palladion episode by means of that colorful and vivid language used in direct descriptions of the hero's attitudes and gestures:

> If knyght or squyer of his compaignie
> Gan for to *syke,* . . . .
> He wolde smyle, and holden it folye.[22]

A moment later, Troilus—not Troilo—displays that very symptom which had excited his mirth:

> . . . . his herte gan to sprede and rise,
> And softe *sighed,* lest men myghte hym here,
> And caughte ayeyn his firste pleyinge chere.[23]

[20] *Fil.,* I, 25.
[21] *Tr. and Cr.,* I, 215–20.
[22] *Ibid.,* I, 191–94.
[23] *Ibid.,* I, 278–80.

This takes us to another aspect of the Palladion scene—the victim's appreciation of the dramatic irony which he discovers has been playing at his expense! Lines 320–29, on Troilus' effort to conceal the fact that he is in love, roughly correspond to *Filostrato,* Book I, stanzas 31–32, but here again Chaucer is more truly interested and gives us three extra stanzas of Troilus' now insincere "japes."[24] He goes farther and credits Pandarus with an equally clear perception of the irony at work. In fact, the wise friend knows so much about mocking Fortune that he had previously been led to expect for Troilus much worse than the "fayre grace" of falling in love with Criseyde.[25] But back of the workings of Destiny, as perceived by Pandarus, we, readers, see the deeper tragic irony of the hero's young life to be lost by the future operations of this "fayre grace." In the same scene this irony combines with a more clearly conveyed and more directly cruel stroke: Pandarus is preaching constancy in love to that same friend whom excess of constancy will ruin; we think of the future scene when he will use his eloquence, but in vain, to dissuade Troilus from fidelity.[26] This is substantially the same in both works, Chaucer's figurative language adding a little vividness here and there.[27]

Very different in nature and subtler in character is our poet's contribution to the touches of dramatic irony resting, even in Boccaccio, on the psychology of a character. The Italian Criseida is eloquent and certainly sincere in her promises of fidelity, both at the time of the lovers' happiness and in their last conversation, where she goes so far as to preach faithfulness to Troilo. Ironical enough, yet of an irony almost shallow compared to that of very similar protestations in the mouth of serious Criseyde.[28] That Chaucer developed the character primarily for its own sake cannot be questioned; that he was perfectly aware of the bearing of such development on the irony of the action will appear more clearly when, in the next

[24] *Ibid.,* I, 330–50.

[25] *Ibid.,* I, 906–10.

[26] *Tr. and Cr.,* IV, 401–27, and *Fil.,* IV, 48–49. In that scene, one more irony is felt: the half-hearted philosophy of Pandarus will apply to the case of the lovers' separation, but the other way round.

[27] E.g., *Tr. and Cr.,* Bk. I, l. 969, corresponding to *Fil.,* Bk. II, st. 24, l. 3.

[28] It must be stated here that I do not accept J. S. Craydon's view of the character of Criseyde ("Defense of Criseyde," *P.M.L.A.,* XLIV [1929], 141–77). This view, with its main basis, viz., the reconstructed chronology of Book V, would bring in two new strokes of dramatic irony: (1) "Troilus, in accepting Cassandra's interpretation of his dream, compels Criseyde to abandon her efforts to escape from the camp"; (2) "Incited to pursue his supposed successful rival with murderous intent, he [Troilus] finally inflicts upon him the *wyde wowndes* that cause Criseyde, for pity, to finally yield her heart to Diomede. Troilus is eventually betrayed, and Diomede's years of devotion rewarded, as the result of Troilus' almost successful effort to revenge the betrayal which he wrongly believed to have already occurred" (*op. cit.,* p. 176).

section, we shall note several strokes created by Chaucer around this same motif of Criseyde's "trouthe."

In that same parting scene, Criseida's care for her reputation makes her reject Troilo's plan (of leaving Troy together), with the result of a rather more serious blot on her honor. Boccaccio neither insists nor comments, but the bitter dramatic irony of the heroine's care of her good name did not escape Chaucer's attention. Hence that poignant scene of her remorse, where Chaucer throws such harsh ironical light on her former niceties, making her express her miserable regrets at having lost indeed her "name of trouthe in love."[29] The interesting and somewhat surprising fact is that so much of this remorse scene should come straight from Benoît de Sainte-Maure.[30]

As further strokes of dramatic irony found both in the *Filostrato* and the *Troilus* we might mention the hero's farewell words to Criseyde, which words, overheard by Diomede, will cause the catastrophe, or the definiteness of the expectations of Troilus during the first ten days of Criseyde's absence. But rather than dwell on motifs treated much like those that we have already analyzed, it may be well to ask whether there is in the *Filostrato* any dramatic irony that has not passed into Chaucer's work. We should not be far from the truth answering in the negative, for I find only three omissions, two of which can perhaps be accounted for:

*a*) Stanzas 22–23 of Book I, *Filostrato,* give us Troilo's severe reflections on the levity of women. There is some irony in the fact that it is precisely that inconstancy—on account of which he thinks himself so very wise in avoiding love—that will be the cause of his undoing. But Chaucer, for reasons that do not seem to have anything to do with dramatic irony, had made up his mind to represent Troilus as a younger man without previous experience in love.

*b*) Criseida, having argued against the suggestion of leaving the city with Troilo, concludes with the words: *"Per che andar mi conviene con Diomede."*[31] After her emphatic protestations of fidelity, this seemingly accidental mention of the name of her future lover is a stroke that Chaucer can hardly have failed to notice. But he could not make his Criseyde mention Diomede here without previously informing us, as does Boccaccio,[32] that the ambassador sent from the Greek camp will be Diomede.

---

[29] *Tr. and Cr.,* V, 1051–71.

[30] See K. Young, *The Origin and Development of the Story of Troilus and Criseyde* (Ch. Soc., 1908), p. 135.

[31] *Fil.,* Bk. IV, st. 130, l. 5.

[32] At least in the text edited by Baroni (*Fil.,* IV, 13). In the edition of Moutier and in that of Griffin and Myrick, Criseida's mention of Diomede is quite unprepared.

He avoids both mentions of the name, sacrificing dramatic irony to achieve another effect by the more sudden, more startling disclosure of the fact that the ambassador already waiting to take Criseyde to the camp is that interesting and puzzling Diomede, of whom Chaucer, and Chaucer alone,[33] has previously told us that he is to succeed Troilus in the favors of Criseyde.

*c*) The Italian Troilo objects to a holiday at Sarpedon's because he fears that Criseida may return during his absence, i.e., before the appointed time. The corresponding scene in Chaucer is one of the not perfectly finished portions[34] of the fifth book; we should not try to guess any reason why dramatic irony has been left out.

To summarize this section: besides taking over most of the dramatic irony present in the *Filostrato* and translating Boccaccio's somewhat insistent direct comments, Chaucer often added illustrations of his own and sharpened contrasts by the use of his picturesque figurative language. In some instances, more interesting and more definite characterization has been found to throw much stronger ironical light on contrasts already present in Boccaccio's work. Yet Chaucer's delight in exploiting the new device did not prevent him from weighing against it the promises of other methods of narrative presentation and, in two cases, of giving up an effect of dramatic irony found in the *Filostrato.* We shall have to remark again on the complete freedom from anything systematic or mechanical in Chaucer's use of the device.

2. *Dramatic irony added to situations supplied by the "Filostrato."*—We have seen Chaucer taking over from the *Filostrato,* along with definite instances of dramatic irony, Boccaccio's characteristic method of calling his readers' attention to such irony. We shall now find our poet extending his master's method of presentation to an ironical contrast for which the *Filostrato* offered a favorable frame but which was not even suggested in it. The Trojans are discussing the exchange of Criseyde against Antenor:

> The noyse of peple up sterte thanne at ones
> As breme as blase of straw iset on fire;
> For infortune it wolde, for the nones,
> They sholden hire confusioun desire.
> "Ector," quod they, "what goost may yow enspire,
> This womman thus to shilde, and don us leese
> Daun Antenor?—a wrong wey now ye chese,—
>
> "That is so wys and ek so bold baroun,
> And we han nede of folk, as men may se."[35]

[33] *Tr. and Cr.,* IV, 11; cf. *Fil.,* III, 94.

[34] Lines 428–31 are not quite the expected wording after lines 400–403.

[35] *Tr. and Cr.,* IV, 183–91.

There is, of course, irony in Hector's rôle: he does not know that he is preaching his brother's cause, and he is protecting Criseyde in a way quite different from his intended one. This little comedy is Chaucer's contribution. But for the other, very different, irony of the episode, viz., the insistence of the Trojans on regaining their captured hero, who will prove a traitor, the material was supplied by Benoît de Sainte-Maure. In Boccaccio the same exchange of prisoners has to take place, but there is no allusion to the future rôle of Antenor in the fall of the city. Chaucer is less afraid of a little digression; and, besides, the powers of Destiny at work in the Trojan war are part of that fatalistic background so important in his eyes. The desired ironical effect might have been achieved by lines 185–86 quoted above, supplemented by the explanation of lines 204–5, "For he was after traitour to the town Of Troye," but Chaucer instinctively adopts the manner in which his master Boccaccio would have written about Antenor had he been interested in the war setting:

> O Juvenal, lord! soth is thy sentence,
> That litel wyten folk what is to yerne,
> That they ne fynde in hir desir offence;
> For cloude of errour lat hem nat discerne
> What best is; and, lo, here ensaumple as yerne.
> *This folk desiren now deliveraunce*
> *Of Antenor, that broughte hem to meschaunce.*
>
> For he was after traitour to the town
> Of Troye; allas, they quytte hym out to rathe!
> O nyce world, lo thy discrecioun![36]

Nothing could be more like a translation from Boccaccio. And yet, in *Troilus and Criseyde,* we find several interesting examples of entirely objective presentation of dramatic irony, a method which in later work will completely replace that of the Italian master. For instance in Book III, lines 374–76, there is a significant change in an oath put in the mouth of the hero. Boccaccio wrote:

> "Ma nondimen per quello Dio ti giuro,
> Che 'l cielo e 'l mondo egualmente governa,
> E s'io non venga nelle man del duro
> *Agamennon, che* ..."[37]

Chaucer "translates":

> "And if I lye, *Achilles* with his spere
> Myn herte cleve, . . . ."

Rossetti comments: "Perhaps he [Chaucer] was guided by the reflection

---

[36] *Tr. and Cr.,* IV, 197–206.

[37] *Fil.,* Bk. III, st. 15, ll. 1–4.

that Troilus did actually, at last, fall by the hand of Achilles."[38] The "perhaps" might be left out; what we have is a deliberate and powerful stroke of tragic irony. Chaucer knows that no comment is called for.

Another instance of irony so lightly touched upon as to escape many readers is pointed out in Dr. Root's note to line 842, Book V: while, in Boccaccio, Diomede's long conversation with Criseida—a rather serious step in his courtship—occurs on her fourth day in the Greek camp, Chaucer gains in irony by placing the same scene on that tenth day on which Criseyde was to come back to Troy, and Troilus most eagerly and hopefully keeps waiting for her outside the walls of the city. The coincidence is there. We can stop to ponder about mocking Fate if we wish.

Several such quick touches of irony are grafted by Chaucer on the theme of fidelity. First, the irony of Troilus' faith in Criseyde. Pandarus has argued that "Absence of hire shal dryve hire out of herte." Troilus hardly listens:

> "This lechecraft, or heeled thus to be,
> Were wel sittyng, if that I were a fend,
> To traysen a wight *that trewe is unto me!*"[39]

Again, after the separation, he feels sorry for her,

> "For wel I woot as yvele as I ye fare."[40]

> "How shal she don ek, sorwful creature?
> For tendernesse how shal she ek sustene
> Swich wo for me?"[41]

As to Criseyde, if the irony of her vows of fidelity is developed from Boccaccio (see preceding section, p. 17), the deeper and subtler irony resulting from her half intellectual, half religious reverence for "trouthe" in the abstract is entirely Chaucer's contribution. The striking lines in this

---

[38] W. M. Rossetti, *Chaucer's Troylus and Criseyde* (Ch. Soc., 1873), p. 118.

[39] *Tr. and Cr.,* IV, 436–38.

[40] *Ibid.,* V, 238.

[41] *Ibid.,* V, 241–43. Perhaps we should mention in this connection a stanza that does not answer our definition of dramatic irony, but produces an impression very similar to that of the three passages just quoted; I mean the lines in which Troilus expresses his fears of the refined and cultured Greeks as possible rivals (IV, 1485–91). His words do not create any contrast with the rest of the story. On the contrary, they are almost too much to the point, and, exactly because we feel that the speaker has no conception of how terribly appropriate they are, we half suspect the action of those same mocking forces that are creating irony of circumstances all through the tragedy. (In the Italian, Troilo considers only the possibility of Criseida's father choosing a Greek husband for her. See *Fil.,* IV, 142, corresponding to *Tr. and Cr.,* IV, 1471–74.) For similar effects, see also *Tr. and Cr.,* III, 1641 ("in my gylt"), and V, 651 ("if al the world be trewe").

respect are those in which Criseyde, whose name is to become synonymous with faithlessness, tells Troilus how "moral vertu grounded upon trouthe"[42] caused her to love him. There is no scorn, no harshness in our smile, only pity for Criseyde, even respect perhaps, accompanied by intellectual uneasiness. Are even our deepest feelings mere toys in the hands of some whimsical force? For this beautiful touch the field has been prepared by interestingly free manipulation of Boccaccio's poem. In the corresponding scene of the *Filostrato,*[43] it is Troilo who enumerates the virtues that he found in Criseida; in other words, it is the poet who pays an almost direct compliment to Maria d'Aquino. Had Chaucer simply added fidelity to the list of those virtues, he would only have repeated here an ironical motif—Troilus' faith in Criseyde—which we have found sufficiently stressed in passages previously mentioned. By reversing the parts and making Criseyde praise Troilus for his "trouthe," he not only created an opportunity for subtle characterization of his heroine, but, from this characterization, he derived dramatic irony of much greater depth and complexity. Is it too bold to suggest appreciation of this type of dramatic irony as one of the reasons for the reversal of parts?

With similar dramatic irony derived from Criseyde's interest in "trouthe," another motif, derived from the character of Troilus, is combined in Book II, lines 786–88. While Criseida argued only from the frailty of husbands' love to the wisdom of taking a lover,[44] Criseyde applies similar considerations to men in general: she, the future mistress of Diomede, hesitates to answer the love of Troilus because he might not be true to her!

In the vows of fidelity lavished by Criseida upon her lover, we read:

> "Però sicuro vivi del mio amore,
> Il qual mai per altrui più non provai."[45]

Chaucer translated:

> "Beth glad, forthy, and lyve in sikernesse;
> Thus seyde I nevere or now, ne shal to mo."[46]

By this deft little change—simply a reference to both past and future, instead of past only—Chaucer forces us to keep in mind the unhappy issue, and this clearer anticipation throws upon the whole scene a stronger ironical light.

Also in Criseyde's promises of fidelity during the lovers' last meeting—the irony of these promises has been previously mentioned[47] as derived

---

[42] *Tr. and Cr.,* IV, 1672.
[43] *Fil.,* IV, 164–65.
[44] *Ibid.,* II, 73–74.
[45] *Ibid.,* III, 50.
[46] *Tr. and Cr.,* III, 1513–14.
[47] See p. 17.

from Boccaccio—two new strokes must be noted in the present section: Criseyde's violent curse of her future self, a curse that reminds us of Oedipus:

> "For thilke day that I for cherisshyng
> Or drede of fader, or for other wight,
> Or for estat, delit, or for weddyng,
> Be fals to you, my Troilus, my knyght,
> Saturnes doughter, Juno, thorugh hire myght,
> As wood as Athamante do me dwelle
> Eternalich in Stix, the put of helle."[48]

The second such addition is Criseyde's (accidental?) use of a formula quite simple, almost colorless:

> "and *or ye cause fynde,*
> For goddes love, so beth me naught unkynde."[49]

And, finally, to this theme of fidelity as emphasized all through the *Troilus,* we are indebted for the intensity of this most lamentable and piercing irony of Criseyde's life: she has not kept her faith to Troilus, to

> "the gentileste
> That evere was, and oon the worthieste,"[50]

but she is going to be true to this "sudden" Diomede:

> "But syn I se ther is no bettre way,
> And that to late it is now for to rewe,
> To Diomede algate I wol be trewe."[51]

Will he be true to her? The reader feels that the irony of Fate is playing upon the deepest feelings of poor Criseyde in a very subtle way, that the whole tragedy is probably not over. The pathos of Criseyde's words is dependent upon all we know of her character, but the words themselves—one has to look at it twice before one believes it—are actually translated, like most of the scene, from Benoît de Sainte-Maure:

> "E que me vaut, se m'en repent?
> En ço n'a mais recovrement.
> Serai donc a cestui leiaus ..."[52]

More examples could be added, but those already discussed have illustrated sufficiently, not only the keen sense with which Chaucer detected new chances for dramatic irony in the material presented to him, but also

---

[48] *Tr. and Cr.,* IV, 1534–40.
[49] *Ibid.,* IV, 1651–52.
[50] *Ibid.,* V, 1056–57.
[51] *Ibid.,* V, 1069–71.
[52] *Roman de Troie,* edited by Léopold Constans (Société des Anciens Textes Français, Paris, 1904–12), Vol. III, ll. 20265–68.

his early emancipation from Boccaccio's tutelage: light touches and objective presentation are found more frequently than typically Boccaccian comments, and the newly introduced ironies have a subtlety and intensity unparalleled in the *Filostrato*. Their effectiveness is largely dependent on a character delineation which is mostly Chaucer's own.

3. *Dramatic irony in episodes created by Chaucer.*—Three episodes deserve our attention: (*a*) the garden scene in Book II, (*b*) the scene at the house of Deiphebus in the same book, and (*c*) the episode of the rainy night in Book III.

*a*) In the garden scene (II, 813–910), though both the garden setting and much of the song of Antigone may have been suggested by later episodes in the *Filostrato*,[53] the dramatic irony of the scene under consideration comes from a new situation which is Chaucer's entirely. Criseyde has just been debating the question whether she should accept the love of Troilus. Shall she forfeit her liberty? Love is such a stormy life, men are so untrue and wicked tongues so biting.[54] Just at the psychological moment the enraptured song of Antigone bursts forth. The irony lies in the fact that, without suspecting her words of having any special bearing on the situation, the singer takes up one by one all the scruples of Criseyde[55] until she concludes:

> "Al dredde I first to love hym to bigynne,
> Now woot I wel, ther is no peril inne."[56]

In the conversation that follows, Antigone still unconsciously advocates the cause of Troilus until Criseyde gradually "wax somwhat able to converte." The delightful irony of this scene answers more than one purpose: it heightens our feeling that Criseyde is irresistibly led by a sort of conspiracy of circumstances and greatly intensifies our interest in the mental state of the heroine. Also, its altogether pleasant character contributes to the delicate atmosphere of optimism, of genial and youthful yearning for life, which pervades the whole scene and makes it stand unique in the somber tragedy as the lovely garden of Criseyde against the dire background of the war.

*b*) The episode of the dinner at the house of Deiphebus (II, 1394 ff.)

---

[53] See K. Young, *The Origin and Development of the Story of Troilus and Criseyde* (Ch. Soc., 1908), pp. 173–76.

[54] *Tr. and Cr.*, II, 771–805.

[55] Compare, in Criseyde's reflections, ll. 771–74 with Antigone's song, ll. 855–57, 851; ll. 775–79 with l. 833; ll. 780–81 with l. 837; ll. 785–86 with ll. 855–60, 865; ll. 786–98 with ll. 841–43. B. Jefferson (*op. cit.*, p. 127) very appropriately compares this song of Antigone with those of Pippa in Browning.

[56] *Tr. and Cr.*, II, 874–75.

is Chaucer's invention: a masterly plot due partly to the genuine kindness of Pandarus, partly to his intense delight in the ironical situations he creates, very specially in the blindness of the characters. Deiphebus is to be the main one:

> "Now," quod Pandare, "or houres twyes twelve,
> He shal the ese, *unwist of it hym selve*."[57]

Troilus soon learns the details of the skilful "blinding" of Deiphebus.[58] It has, indeed, been more than successful, for Pandarus has been given the unanticipated pleasure of this piece of superfluous advice:

> "Speke thow thi self also to Troilus
> On my byhalve, and prey hym with us dyne."[59]

"Of his owen curteisie," Deiphebus comes in person to invite Criseyde—and this in the presence of Pandarus, whose repressed laughter we can imagine. On the ironies of the further conversation between Deiphebus and Troilus, Chaucer insists in the characteristic Boccaccian style of the afternoon party:

> God woot, that he [Troilus] it graunted anon right,
> To ben hire fulle frend with al his myght;
> But swich a nede was to preye hym thenne,
> As for to bidde a wood man for to renne.[60]

The unsuspecting guests gather:

> But god and Pandare wist al what this mente.[61]

Different remedies are suggested for the illness of Troilus[62] in the presence of Pandarus and Criseyde, who quietly thinks: "best koude I yit ben his leche."[63] No less serious is the argument on Polyphete's supposed attacks upon Criseyde. All this while, Troilus is lying "sick" in his room. It is Eleyne who helps Pandarus out;[64] once in the room, it is she again who, in her "goodly softe wyse," starts the topic of Criseyde and of the protection which Troilus should not refuse her.[65] Troilus promises:

> "I wol right fayn with al my myght ben oon,
> Have god my trouthe, hire cause to sustene."
> "Good thrift have ye," quod Eleyne, the queene.[66]

---

57 *Ibid.*, II, 1399–1400. 58 *Ibid.*, II, 1496.

59 *Ibid.*, II, 1457–58. 60 *Ibid.*, II, 1551–54. 61 *Ibid.*, II, 1561.

62 The feigned illness of Troilus may have been suggested by scenes near the end of the Italian poem (*Fil.*, VII, 83–85) not otherwise used by Chaucer (see Cummings, *op. cit.*, pp. 59–60). There was no irony there.

63 *Tr. and Cr.*, II, 1582. 64 *Ibid.*, II, 1625–27.

65 *Ibid.*, II, 1671–80. 66 *Ibid.*, II, 1685–87.

In the rest of the episode—the pretexts invented by Pandarus to get Deiphebus and Eleyne out of the room, etc.—there is excellent comedy but no irony of action.

*c*) Pandarus' next creation is the plot of the rainy night (III, 512 ff.). The suggestion for the jealous fit of Troilus seems to come from two scenes in the *Filocolo,* where the irony, however, is about as simple as possible: a lover's real suspicion is groundless. In Chaucer, the fact that Troilus' jealousy is feigned[67] adds a little irony to the part of Criseyde, who takes it all so seriously, and also makes us think of the future episodes where Troilus will have a very real ground for more than mere suspicions.

Apart from the Epilogue and the soliloquy on free will, the three episodes just studied are the only additions of any length to the poem of Boccaccio. They show how continually Chaucer was keeping in mind the resources of the irony of action, and they point to comedy, delicate or highly spirited, as a most promising field for his future use of the device.

## Conclusions

As dramatic irony is used frequently and with strong emphasis in the *Filostrato,* readapting the Italian poem was the best possible early training in handling the device. But Chaucer went much farther than to rework the *Filostrato* with eloquent appreciation of the dramatic irony in it, much farther than learning Boccaccio's method of commenting rather insistently on the ironies of Fate, farther even than acquiring the master's talent for detecting or creating tragic or amusing irony; he developed a sense for new effects, for irony of a subtler character than any emphasized in the *Filostrato,* touches often too subtle and indefinite for any comment on his part to be desirable. Thus we find in the *Troilus* several interesting examples of a light, reticent, completely objective method of presenting the ironies of action. Other masters will encourage Chaucer to cultivate this method and abandon the other completely.

---

[67] I see no ground for J. Craydon's view that this scene reveals the jealous disposition of Troilus; see *P.M.L.A.,* XLIV (1929), 159–61.

# III. CHAUCER'S FABLIAUX

Under this heading we shall include, irrespective of the literary genre to which their sources may have belonged, the tales treated by Chaucer in the fabliau spirit or, let us say, in a spirit a little more suggestive of the fabliaux than of other literary genres.

In only one case can we compare a fabliau of Chaucer with its source, or at least with a version very close to that source: the French *Le meunier et les II clers* presents, in common with the *Reeve's Tale,* a sufficient number of specific, non-indispensable features to establish beyond any doubt a close relationship (quite acceptable as regards time and locality) between the English and the earlier French version. This degree of similarity does not exist between the other *Canterbury Tales* fabliaux and any of their often quite numerous analogues. Those analogues, however, do prove that Chaucer did not create his plots out of nothing, i.e., that lost forms of the stories must be postulated as sources of his tales. In our attempt to determine the amount of dramatic irony supplied by the sources, we shall accordingly find ourselves quite often on rather uncertain grounds. Fortunately the French *Le meunier et les II clers* is a perfect representative of the fabliau genre with all its virtues, all its limitations, and—especially interesting for us—with its typically fabliau love of a certain kind of dramatic irony and its no less typical treatment of it. For this reason it seems advisable to open our study of Chaucer's fabliaux with a comparison of the irony of action in the *Reeve's Tale* and in *Le meunier.* On the results of this study we shall frequently have to lean when we come to the more delicate questions of our poet's relation to his lost sources.

## THE "REEVE'S TALE"

Though the story of *Le meunier et les II clers* can be considered as the source of the *Reeve's Tale,* we shall have to keep in mind that neither of our two slightly different versions of this fabliau can claim to be the unique source known to Chaucer. We shall refer to, and quote from, the version of the Hamilton MS 257, as printed by H. Varnhagen in *Englische Studien.*[1]

---

[1] *Engl. Stud.,* IX (1886), 241 ff. The text is in a rather poor state, but this version, in many respects, seems closer to Chaucer's source (or to one of his sources) than does the better preserved version published in *Or. and An.,* p. 102, and by Montaiglon et Raynaud, *Recueil général et complet des fabliaux,* V, 83 ff. I have treated this question in *J.E.G.P.,* XXIX (1930), 473–88.

The theme is that of which the French trouvères never tired—the deceiver deceived. In other words, dramatic irony is the very essence and spirit of the plot as Chaucer had it from his model. Let us see how far and in what way the ironical resources of this theme are exploited in the French fabliau and in the *Reeve's Tale,* confronting the two versions as often as possible.

As our French rimer, in this particular case, happens to open the story without any remark on deceivers deceived or foolers befooled, the second act of the comedy cannot be anticipated, and the irony of the miller's success can be enjoyed only by retrospection or on a second reading. In the *Canterbury Tales,* Osewold the Reeve, who wants to repay Robin the Miller with his own coin, announces in his prologue a tale of a cheated miller. From the first we accordingly rejoice in anticipations of Simkin's coming misfortunes, a superiority over the French texts as we have them, but a feature entirely in keeping with fabliau practices.

Chaucer's next step is the preparation of ironical effects by means of elaborate characterization. Some of the details in his leisurely introduction of Simkin and his family have, of course, a comic value independent of the rest of the story, partly because the Reeve is drawing a portrait which skilfully suggests the Miller of the general Prologue.[2] But most of what is said is calculated to strike as strong a contrast as possible with the amusing dénouement: the miller swaggers about armed with daggers and knives that he may look the more ridiculous when beaten by the clerks and receiving the decisive blow from his wife; he is jealous and foolishly proud of having married a woman of "noble kin" brought up in a nunnery that we may laugh the more at his misfortunes; his wife is "digne as water in a dich" and his daughter is to be married "hye In-to som worthy blood of auncestrye" in order that their surrender to the clerks may appear more ridiculous and out of keeping with former expectations; and, finally, Simkin is not one of those common uninteresting thieves who would steal just for the sake of profit—he is an artist, a dilettante, one who knows all the scale from "curteous" to "outrageous" theft and enjoys the practice of his art a hundred times more than the possession of a few pounds of meal. How very much more captivating to watch the process by which such a man is to be caught in his own net! For we know he will be. And indeed we soon learn that the clerks are a match for Simkin. No necessity, not even a sensible desire to put an end to the miller's "outrageous" stealing, has set Aleyn and John on the way, but

[2] See W. M. Hart, "*The Reeve's Tale,* A Comparative Study of Chaucer's Narrative Art," *P.M.L.A.*, XXIII (1908), 10–11.

> only for hir mirthe and revelrye,
> Up-on the wardeyn bisily they crye,
> To yeve hem leve but a litel stounde
> To goon to mille and seen hir corn y-grounde;
> And hardily, they dorste leye hir nekke,
> The miller shold nat stele hem half a pekke
> Of corn by sleighte, ne by force hem reve.[3]

This is a game in craft and wiliness, alluring in the clerks' eyes and promising in ours for exactly the same reason: characteristics of the chief participants lead us to expect a fight at close quarters and a dénouement bound to strike an amusing contrast with the miller's expectations.

Our two friends arrive at the mill and Aleyn greets the miller:

> "al hayl, Symond, y-fayth;
> How fares thy faire doghter and thy wyf?"[4]

Possibly we had already guessed what kind of bad luck was awaiting the miller in the Reeve's retort to the story of Alison and Nicholas? In any case, at least on a second reading, we find Aleyn's polite greeting amusingly ironical because so perfectly harmless, not only in surface meaning but in intention.

The conversation takes its natural turn: John will watch the corn go in—he never had the chance before—and Aleyn will see the meal fall into the trough—that will be his "disport." Such a show of purely theoretical interest in the processes of grinding is too simple a trick for Simkin:

> "The more queynte crekes that they make,
> The more wol I stele whan I take."[5]

The irony is twofold: the clerks who pride themselves on their cleverness are giving the miller a sort of challenge the result of which will be the theft of the meal, but at the same time Simkin's readiness to accept the challenge will make him the only dupe in the end. The second irony is of course the stronger. In the miller's smile there is more than anticipatory delight in the success of his own cunning; there is the delicate pleasure of getting the better of two clerks in spite of "al the sleighte in hir philosophye," the triumph—or revenge—of native common sense and of experience over bookish knowledge, a triumph in which it is hard to tell whether the vanity of the individual or the half-defensive pride of class finds the larger gratification—temporarily!

The next lines express the miller's slyness by perfect pantomime:

> Out at the dore he gooth ful prively,
> Whan that he saugh his tyme, softely; . . . .
> And to the hors he gooth him faire and wel;
> He strepeth of the brydel right anon.[6]

---

[3] A. 4005–11. [4] A. 4022–23. [5] A. 4051–52. [6] A. 4057–63.

We feel the exultation of success in every one of the miller's gestures. Presently it will burst out into open triumph:

> "Yet can a miller make a clerkes berd
> For al his art; now lat hem goon hir weye.
> Lo wher they goon, ye, lat the children pleye;
> They gete him nat so lightly, by my croun!"[7]

In exact proportion to the joy of Simkin rises our anticipatory pleasure in whatever misfortune awaits him at the hands of his present victims. To this general irony a more definite touch is added on a second reading, where Simkin's wish to have the flour baked into a cake[8] derives a special flavor from a later episode in which our hero is to appear less triumphant.

John and Aleyn have caught the horse at last, but their sigh of relief is not pure joy: not only do they come back "wery and weet, as beste is in the reyn," but, having started the game for the game's sake, they cannot be blind to the dramatic irony of which they have been victims:

> "Allas," quod John, "the day that I was born!
> Now are we drive til hething and til scorn.
> Our corn is stole, men wil us foles calle,
> Bathe the wardeyn and our felawes alle,
> And namely the miller; weylaway!"[9]

They find Simkin comfortably seated by the fire and not even repressing his self-satisfaction. This is not likely to reconcile them to their fortunes. More than ever, they deserve the epithet which Chaucer generally applies to the dupes of his fabliaux: they are "sely clerkes,"[10] lamentably "sely" in their own judgment and exquisitely so in the miller's. One humiliation more has to be brooked: they must pray for "herberwe . . . . as for hir peny." The miller's witty answer is the climax of his triumph over university men as such:

> "Myn hous is streit, but ye han lerned art;
> Ye conne by argumentes make a place
> A myle brood of twenty foot of space.
> Lat see now if this place may suffyse,
> Or make it roum with speche, as is youre gyse."[11]

Simkin's direct conscious irony is excellent, but in our eyes the richest fun of the passage lies in its unconscious, i.e., its dramatic, irony that turns the joke against the joker. For these very dimensions of his one room which the clerks are ironically invited to argue larger are to be distinctly more detrimental to Simkin than to his guests.

---

[7] A. 4096–99. [8] A. 4094. [9] A. 4109–13.

[10] A. 4090, 4100, 4108. "Sely" does not mean "silly," but "simple."

[11] A. 4122–26.

Having been so entirely successful, the miller can relax and turn hospitable, simply assuming an ironically protective attitude when he ties the horse that "it sholde nat gon loos." Once more we smile with Simkin, though for a very different reason: we begin to foresee the ultimate consequences of that wonderful ruse the recollection of which gives our hero such delight.

In this survey of the first half of the *Reeve's Tale* we have had to set the French fabliau aside, the *Reeve's Tale* being too independent in plot and too rich in details for a step-by-step comparison of the two versions.[12] The fabliau, of course, supplied the main irony, that of the miller's temporary success. But to our trouvère this incongruity inherent in the plot was entirely satisfying and sufficient. The joke was in the story. Hence a complete disregard of characterization as a possible method for sharpening contrasts. A few quick notations are needed to prepare for the action: the miller is presented as the typical robber. We are also told that he is in the habit of locking his daughter in a bin at night, a detail which is in no way indispensable for the preparation of what follows.[13] Perhaps a desire to create a strong contrast between expectations and realizations (along with unquestionable pleasure in the picturesque detail of the bin) may have caused the introduction of this feature here? But a true jongleur should not go much farther: of the miller's feelings in the matter, of his being or not being jealous of his wife, not a word. The two clerks are, if possible, still less individualized; the dramatic irony which in the first part of the *Reeve's Tale* plays at their expense for trying to outwit Simkin is not even conceivable where they prosaically come to the mill to have their corn ground. Finally, nothing in the French fabliau corresponds to those half-hints by which Chaucer made us foresee the second act of his comedy: no anticipation of the dénouement by means of any introduction, not even a mention of the miller's daughter before the stealing episode is over—nothing that could make us feel, on the first reading, the irony of the thief's temporary success.

The trouvère's appreciation of different ironical contrasts is more clearly perceptible in the second part of the story. Here, the *Reeve's Tale* is closer to the fabliau (at least as far as the intrigue goes), so that a comparison of details with details is possible.

---

[12] In the French, the miller is determined to steal as much as he can. When he sees the clerks coming, he goes and hides in a wood. One of the clerks goes after him, then the second clerk after the first, leaving wheat and mare unguarded. The miller then comes back and, with the help of his wife, conceals everything in his barn before the victims reappear.

[13] Not even for the iron-ring deception of the fabliau.

In the French, the clerks have had a glimpse of the stolen goods hidden by the miller,[14] with the result that at least one of the two young men feels afraid and cautious. On English Aleyn the effect of a similar understanding of the situation is just the opposite:

> "Som esement has lawe y-shapen us;
> For John, ther is a lawe that says thus,
> That gif a man in a point be y-greved,
> That in another he sal be releved."[15]

Hearing him state so clearly the abstract principle on which he acts, we smile, remembering Simkin's opinion of such "philosophy" as foolish and harmless!

Simkin's wife is on the point of entering her own bed:

> "Allas!" quod she, "I hadde almost misgoon;
> I hadde almost gon to the clerkes bed.
> Ey, *benedicite!* thanne hadde I foule y-sped."[16]

Saying so, she gropes her way to John. In the French fabliau the irony of the situation is exactly the same and striking enough in itself. It is not emphasized by any reflection of the woman. All we know about her thoughts and feelings is what we can infer from her physical movements.[17] The corresponding passage of the fabliau *De Gombert et des II clers*[18] is verbally closer to the *Reeve's Tale,* though here it is the husband who gropes for the cradle intentionally misplaced in his absence:

> Quant il n'a le berçuel trové,
> Lors se tient à musart prové,
> Bien cuide avoir voie marie.
> "Li maufez, dist-il, me tarie,
> Quar en cest lit gisent mi oste!"[19]

---

[14] This feature of the Hamilton MS version (ll. 167–70) is not paralleled in the other text.

[15] A. 4179–82.

[16] A. 4218–20.

[17] Ll. 231–40.

[18] Montaiglon et Raynaud, *Recueil,* I, 238 ff. This fabliau, like the two German versions (Varnhagen, *op. cit.,* pp. 240–41 and 256–59), *Decam.,* IX, 6, and *Le berceau* of La Fontaine (*Contes et nouvelles,* II, 3), relates only the second part of the *Rv. T.* or *Le meunier,* i.e., the cradle story without the miller's theft.

[19] Ll. 95–99. This is the only passage for which the fabliau *De Gombert* offers a better parallel than *Le meunier.* Chaucer is very likely to have known the cradle story in this isolated form. He may also have adapted the whole passage from a lost version of *Le meunier,* possibly a version close to Boccaccio's source (*"Ma non trovandovi la culla, disse seco stessa: Oimè, cattiva me, vedi quel che io faceva! in fe di Dio, che io me n'andava dirittamente nel letto degli osti miei"*). But did either Chaucer or Boccaccio need any suggestion for this monologue of the woman?

When Aleyn in his turn mistakes one bed for the other, Chaucer puts into his mouth words similar to those of the wife, not only stressing the irony of the situation, but adding an amusing touch: the clerk's quickness in accounting for his "toty" head, while in fact he just starts "misgoing."[20] For this monologue no extant analogue has any parallel.

This mistake of the clerk creates an incongruous situation of the kind that our trouvères loved. And really there is an amusing shock and an effective minute of tension when we hear the girl's lover tell his story to the very man from whom he should have endeavored to keep it secret. But, to the reader of Montaiglon's *Recueil,* the trick appears as somewhat outworn, or at any rate too easy,[21] and we feel thankful to Chaucer for having compressed the revelations of Aleyn in the six lines necessary to carry the intrigue forward.[22] That the French miller should listen to a confession of fifteen lines before seizing the clerk by the throat is of course quite unnatural. But the trouvères will pay any price, including remorseless sacrifice of verisimilitude, for the pleasure of dwelling on an incongruous, absurd situation. The Boccaccio of the *Decameron* often follows their example, but Chaucer's stricter realism puts him on his guard against prolonged unnatural mistakes.

The concrete result of the clerk's confession is the same in both versions, but Chaucer reaps here what he had sown in the first part of his story: instead of *a* miller who is deceived, we have clever Simkin waking up to the result of his masterly piece of cunning; we have dangerous Simkin beaten by his wife!

The denunciation of the miller's theft and the recovery of the stolen goods are excellent dramatic irony in both versions. As a thief, the French miller certainly is caught in a way for which we heartily applaud his wife (his former accomplice!): to his insult,[23] which was not even deserved,

---

[20] A. 4252 ff.

[21] With or without disguise, a person is taken for another (and in some cases that person takes part in long conversations) in *De la borgoise d'Orliens,* Montaiglon, *Recueil,* I, 117; *Des III dames qui trouverent l'anel,* I, 168; *Du chevalier qui fist sa fame confesse,* I, 178; *Des II changeors,* I, 245; *Du prestre et d'Alison,* II, 8; *Le meunier d'Arleux,* II, 31 (first, an ordinary mistake on one side, then a double mistake); *Romanz de un chivaler et de sa dame et de un clerk,* II, 215; *Des tresces,* IV, 67; *Estula,* IV, 87; *De Barat et de Haimet,* IV, 93; *De la dame qui fist entendant son mari qu'il sonjoit,* V, 132.

[22] One coarse touch of irony disappears in this process of condensation: *Le meunier,* ll. 264–66.

[23] In the Hamilton MS, this insult has dropped out of the text, but the woman's answer (ll. 279 ff.) proves that it had been there.

she retorts with her well-founded accusation.[24] In the *Reeve's Tale,* Simkin's theft of half a bushel of meal was too decidedly of the "curteous" kind to prepare for such a violent scene. Chaucer offers us, instead, a situation which is unexpected in the same degree but of a much more subtle and humorous character: Malin, "this wenche thikke and wel y-growen," threatens to shed tears, and gives expression to her tenderness by telling her lover where to find the cake! Perhaps the main point here is the keenly penetrating suggestion of a close connection between sensuality and sentimentalism, but we must not overlook the humorous dramatic irony of the episode. Poor Simkin would have been unfortunate enough—with what he had already lost—in losing this trophy, the cake; but to lose it through the mawkish sentimentality of his betrayed daughter, that same daughter whom he had destined for a rich and noble husband, is to be the victim of an irony almost too wickedly refined. This is comedy somewhat deeper than mere clash of contrasting situations, comedy too complex to have been borrowed from any lost French analogue; it is Chaucer's contribution.

A last difference is significant: while the trouvère, consistently interested in material profit, is content to tell us how the clerks, having recovered their corn, become successful in their business, the greater artist, primarily interested in the dramatic contrast of characters with situations, gives us, in summarizing, something of his secret:

> Thus is the *proude* miller wel y-bete,
> And hath y-lost the grinding of the whete,[25]

—something, yet not too much, not more than the most skilful among the trouvères occasionally provide, not enough to force us into the artist's workshop as Boccaccio would do under similar circumstances:

> Graziose donne, manifesta cosa è tanto più l'arti piacere, quanto più sottile artefice è per quelle artificiosamente beffato. E per ciò, quantunque bellissime cose tutte raccontate abbiate, io intendo di racontárne una, tanto più che alcuna altra déttane da dovervi aggradire, quanto colei che beffata fu era maggior maestra di beffare altrui, che alcuno altro beffato fosse di quegli o di quelle che avete contate.[26]

One often finds the phrase "poetic justice" used in connection with certain fabliaux. There is certainly something like it in the punishment of the miller. But shall we "make ernest of game"? The phrase "poetic justice" seems to put moral values too much in the foreground. Our irresponsible trouvères found equal enjoyment in stories about innocent vic-

---

[24] In the version of the Hamilton MS, where the clerks have had a glimpse at their corn stored away, the only rôle of the woman's denunciation is to give the clerks a plausible reason for beating the miller until he returns the stolen goods.

[25] A. 4313–14.

[26] *Decam.,* VIII, 10.

tims[27] and entirely successful rascals. The dramatic irony of our fabliau and of the *Reeve's Tale* is pure, unadulterated fun.

To state our results, this comparison of the *Reeve's Tale* with a French version close to its source confirms in every respect what we might have inferred from a study of dramatic irony in Chaucer's fabliaux as compared with dramatic irony in the 147 texts of Montaiglon's *Recueil.* Chaucer's debt to the trouvères is enormous and twofold. First, he owes them a number of well-built plots full of such excellent irony of action that they not only recommended themselves for free translation but invited further elaboration. Chaucer indeed developed and enriched these dramatic contrasts, mostly by a character drawing that lay entirely outside the lines of fabliau tradition. No doubt his interest in human nature and psychological truth would have made him develop the types of nearly any of the French fabliaux into living individuals, but the choice of the particular features assigned in this case to Simkin and the clerks was determined mostly by a desire to create and stress ironical contrasts. Thus, if dramatic irony depends for its effectiveness on good characterization, characterization, in its turn, owes something to the artist's appreciation of dramatic irony. Chaucer's second great debt to the trouvères is for a lesson in technique. The irony of the French fabliaux is striking because it is excellent in itself, and because of the teller's healthy, communicative delight in a good joke. But the story is left to speak for itself. In all his fabliaux we shall find Chaucer consistently faithful to this technique, of which we had already met several examples in the *Troilus.* More interesting still, even outside of the fabliau genre, we shall no longer hear our poet interpreting ironic situations for us in his former Boccaccian style.

## The "Miller's Tale"

A few facts concerning the lost source, or sources, of the *Miller's Tale* can be established from a study of what extant analogues we have.[28] Our poet certainly was not the first (1) to connect the flood episode with the kiss-and-burn motif, (2) to present the prophecy of the flood as the lover's device to get the husband out of the way, and (3) to end his tale with the cry "water!" which causes the husband's fall. To which we

---

[27] E.g., in *De Gombert et des II clers,* or, among Chaucer's own works, in the *Mil. T.* and the *Sh. T.*

[28] Those facts remain the same no matter which theory we may be inclined to accept concerning the relations of those analogues. See H. Varnhagen, "Zu Chaucers Erzählung des Müllers," *Angl.,* Bd. VII (1884), Anz. 81–84; J. Zupitza's review of A. W. Pollard's edition of the *C.T., Archiv.,* XCIV (1895), 441–45; A. Barnouw, "*The Milleres Tale* van Chaucer," *Handelingen van het zesde Nederlandsche Philologencongres,* pp. 125–39 (Leiden, 1910); or, summarized in English, in *Mod. Lang. Rev.,* VII (1912), 145–48.

may add that the victim in Chaucer's source is not unlikely to have been an old man,[29] and a carpenter.[30] Thus the simplest conceivable form of that source would have at least (1) the irony of the husband's credulity and of his unconscious help to the lovers, and (2) the irony of the lover's shouting of that very word which he should have avoided most carefully. But none of the extant versions betrays any great appreciation of these incongruities. Chaucer's source, as it was probably a French fabliau,[31] is likely to have brought them out with more enjoyment and effectiveness. Yet, on the other hand, as a fabliau again, it is not likely to have developed them in any very complex or subtle way. As we proceed in our survey of the instances of dramatic irony in the tale, we shall venture a few guesses as to the amount of Chaucer's contribution.

The three-line summary given in the Prologue[32] and the emphasis on the jealousy of the husband[33] prepare for ironical situations according to perfect fabliau tradition. Chaucer's own hand is felt more distinctly in a number of finer touches: the carpenter's kind-hearted solicitude for Nicholas, his "lewed man's" philosophy of life, and his deep love for Alison—so many genuine honest feelings, each of which must, by the mockery of fate, cause the "sely" old man to give the lovers quick and efficient help:

> This sely carpenter hath greet merveyle
> Of Nicholas, or what thing mighte him eyle,
> And seyde, "I am adrad, by seint Thomas,
> It stondeth nat aright with Nicholas."[34]

Indeed, it does not "stand aright."

> "God shilde that he deyde sodeynly!"[35]

The carpenter's uneasiness is justified. Has not "hende Nicholas" warned Alison:

---

[29] As in the case of the German Schwankbücher (see Varnhagen, *op. cit.*), which seem to go back to the same originals as Chaucer. (The fact that the same feature is found in the *Zigeunermärchen* constitutes no argument in favor of its presence in Chaucer's source, for the *Zigeunermärchen* itself may be derived from the *Mil. T.* See Barnouw's theory, against Zupitza [*op. cit.*] and Wlislocki [*Zeitschrift für vergleichende Litteraturgeschichte,* II (1889), 192].)

[30] As in Masuccio; see Varnhagen, *op. cit.,* and Barnouw, *op. cit.*

[31] The Flemish version of *Heile van Bersele,* Mr. Barnouw thinks, makes the existence of two different French versions extremely probable.

[32] "For I wol telle a legende and a lyf
Bothe of a Carpenter, and of his wyf,
How that a clerk hath set the wrightes cappe."
—A . 3141–43

[33] A . 3224–32.

[34] A . 3423–26.

[35] A . 3427.

"y-wis, but if ich have my will
For derne love of thee, lemman, I spille."[36]

It is astronomy that has made Nicholas mad:

"A man woot litel what him shal bityde."[37]

The old husband certainly does not!

"Ye, blessed be alwey a lewed man,
That noght but oonly his bileve can!"[38]

"Men sholde nat knowe of *goddes privetee.*"[39]

Is it by chance that Chaucer twice uses this same phrase "goddes privetee," putting it here in the mouth of the victim himself and later[40] in words addressed to him? Or does our poet purposely remind us of A. 3163–64 in the Miller's Prologue:

"An housbond shal nat been inquisitif
Of goddes privetee, nor of his wyf"?

On the threshold of Nicholas' room, this "sely" carpenter recites the magic formula that must expel the wicked spirits—but which wicked spirits does he have in mind, and which should really be expelled?

For this scene of Nicholas' trance none of the extant analogues offers the least parallel.[41] And, indeed, if we remember Montaiglon's *Recueil* and our conclusions about the *Reeve's Tale,* we shall feel that such a long, careful, and humorous introduction to the account of a few coarse tricks suggests no other hand but Chaucer's. This agrees very well with what we would infer from other features of the *Miller's Tale,* especially from its strong local color, an indication of independent treatment of the material.

Of the ironic touches in the next episodes—the prophecy and the preparations for the flood—our poet cannot be called the creator in the same sense, though much of their pathos and humor is due to his undoubtedly independent character drawing:

"allas, my wyf!
And shal she drenche? allas! myn Alisoun!"
For sorwe of this he fil almost adoun.[42]

We cannot read these lines without recalling the feelings of old January for "fresshe May,"[43] but even if we could get rid of that association there

[36] A. 3277–78. [37] A. 3450. [38] A. 3455–56. [39] A. 3454. [40] A. 3558.

[41] The lover is living in the house of the married couple in the *Mil. T.* only.

[42] A. 3522–24.

[43] The parallels are many and very striking: in both cases the lover lives in the house of the married couple; his malady (feigned or real) is due to his love for the pretty wife of the jealous old husband, and the latter's solicitude contributes to bringing the lovers together. The carpenter and January show the same touching devotion

would be in the ridiculous and touching exclamation of the old carpenter a note of human pathos that would still give to this stroke of dramatic irony a unique character in this otherwise purely comical tale. One smile softened with a little pity and mild sadness, and how far we feel from these charming *enfants terribles,* the French jongleurs![44]

Nicholas having given all his directions, the carpenter goes to impart his wisdom to his wife. Chaucer here points out the irony of the situation, though very briefly:

> And to his wyf he tolde his privetee;
> And she was war, and knew it bet than he,
> What al this queynte cast was for to seye.[45]

As the preparations for the flood proceed, we are kept conscious of the half-humorous, half-lamentable contrast of the carpenter's activities with his former efforts to keep his wife "narwe in cage."

In the kiss-and-burn episode, dramatic irony plays at the expense of Alison's two lovers, each in his turn. Absolon comes to the carpenter's house in high spirits. By making him center his hopes on a kiss,[46] Chaucer brings in a little humorous irony that perhaps half redeems the coarseness of what follows. In the last scene, the joke played by circumstances is a joke on the lovers: not only does Nicholas' desire of playing a trick on Absolon cause his own misfortune, but the contrivance of making the carpenter sleep under the roof is followed by just that experience that makes the contriver cry for water. The agent, Absolon, knows nothing about the situation, and the cry is just the one that must inevitably cause the carpenter to discover the true relations of the lovers. Chaucer does not seem to have made any remarkable contribution to the rather complicated web of ironical contrasts in this farce.[47]

---

for their wives (cf. A. 3522–25, 3615–17 with E. 2357–60). The mistake that the first has made in marrying a girl of eighteen is commented upon (A. 3227–30) in words that recall the *Mch. T.* Compare also A. 3398 and E. 1274; A. 3527 and E. 1357; A. 3529–30 and E. 1483–86.

[44] This mood is recalled in A. 3611 ff. In the only analogue where the husband's feelings for his wife are stated, he is characterized as selfish and indifferent: *"Der einfältige Tropf, deme das Leben gleichwol lieber als sein junges Weib . . . ."* ("Lyrum Larum," *Angl.,* II [1879], 135–36).

[45] A. 3603–5.

[46] A. 3679–80, 3682–83, 3716.

[47] He is likely to have contributed the little irony of the smith's jest (A. 3769–70), ironical because more apposite than the jester probably thinks. In most analogues, the character corresponding to Absolon is a smith himself. The fact that he is a clerk, besides making possible the irony just referred to, makes the boast of Nicholas (A. 3299–3300) more amusing: the carpenter will be beguiled, but there will be another clerk to reckon with. The same change allows for the casting of "lovely looks" together with incense (A. 3339–43) as Absolon performs his duties in the church.

## THE "SHIPMAN'S TALE"

The basic irony of the tale—a husband lending money that will be used to buy the favors of his wife—was undoubtedly present in Chaucer's source.[48] But was this the main point, as in the *Shipman's Tale* itself, or was it, as in the *Decameron*[49] and the other close analogues known to us, a more or less secondary feature in a story of a grasping woman whom her lover cleverly tricks out of the money that he had pretended to pay for her love? We have no way of answering the question and shall have to remember both possibilities.

The friendly feelings of a husband toward the lover of his wife is one of the few characterization features on which the trouvères occasionally rely for dramatic irony. Chaucer follows them, but his clever choice of details revealing the unusual delicacy of the hero places the character delineation of the *Shipman's Tale* on an entirely different level from the hasty sketch of conventional types current in the fabliaux. It is delightful to observe our merchant saying "nat ones nay" when the monk claims him "as for cosinage"—which "cosinage" is soon to be treated so airily.[50] Next come the friendly ill-fated invitation, the rich entertaining, and—most ironical of all—the merchant's readiness to comply with the wishes of the monk. A hundred franks?

> "Now sikerly this is a smal requeste;
> My gold is youres, whan that it yow leste.
> And nat only my gold, but my chaffare;
> Take what yow list, god shilde that ye spare."[51]

Such is not the monk's intention!

The merchant's good advice to his wife is similarly calculated to afford the strongest contrast with the real situation:

> "my dere wyf, I thee biseke,
> As be to every wight buxom and meke,
> And for to kepe our good be curious,
> And honestly governe wel our hous.
> *Thou hast y-nough, in every maner wyse,*
> *That to a thrifty houshold may suffyse.*

---

[48] On the many other versions of the same story, see A. C. Lee, *The "Decameron," Its Sources and Analogues* (London, 1909), pp. 246–53; and Henri Régnier, *Œuvres de Jean de La Fontaine* (Paris, 1883–97), IV, 355–57. We might add Raymond Geiger, *Histoires Juives* (Paris, 1927), No. 105, p. 95.

[49] *Decam.*, VIII, 1.

[50] See B. 1338–40:

> "by god and seint Martyn,
> He is na more cosin un-to me
> Than is this leef that hangeth on the tree!"

[51] B. 1473–76.

(We have already heard that she is in debt!)

> Thee lakketh noon *array* ne no vitaille,
> *Of silver in thy purs shaltow nat faille.*[52]

Indeed, we know that she will not lack silver!

The paragraph on the busy life led at Bruges must have been partly intended to stress the already striking contrast of the merchant's sober, somewhat solemn ways with the levity of others at St. Denis during his absence. He comes home well satisfied with the outcome of his journey, which takes us to the excellent scene of his visit to Don John, to my mind a scene of too complex humor, of a comedy that rests too much on emotions and feelings, to have been adapted from any French fabliau without most important contributions on Chaucer's part. The position of the merchant as lender and borrower at the same time, amusing enough in itself, was no doubt introduced primarily for the sake of this scene. In comparatively high spirits, the serious, friendly man is giving Don John a familiarly exhaustive account of his activities. The idea of asking for his hundred franks is so far from him that he does not even think of avoiding what could be taken for an allusion, namely the mention of the coming "chevisaunce." Don John understands it all perfectly well, but here is his chance to settle business matters by means of a shameless little piece of cheating of the woman. In addition, it will give him the unexpected pleasure[53] of slightly annoying the ever kind cousin, pretending to be somewhat hurt by an indelicate hint. Better still, the natural response of the sensitive friend will inevitably bring dramatic irony through the contrast of his scruples with the real situation. This dramatic irony, clear enough on the first reading, becomes more striking when, on a second perusal, we follow the scene remembering the merchant's later account of it:

> "Ye sholde han warned me, er I had gon,
> That he yow hadde an hundred frankes payed
> By redy tokene; and heeld him yvel apayed,
> For that I to him spak of chevisaunce,
> Me semed so, as by his contenaunce."[54]

This exquisite tact of the dupe toward the lover of his wife (her deceiver, too!) constitutes the most subtly humorous contrast of the whole tale, and also one of the most cruel touches in this cruel story. Chaucer had carefully prepared the effect: when the merchant, in the lending scene, politely

---

[52] B. 1431–38.

[53] The monk's delight in irony is shown again in his parting words: "Grete wel our dame, myn owene nece swete" (B. 1553).

[54] B. 1578–82.

asked Don John not to keep his money longer than necessary,[55] Chaucer's main object,[56] I think, was to lend color to the victim's later fears of having offended his friend, and to make a certain coldness on the part of the said friend at least plausible.

The dénouement may be Chaucer's invention. If it is, a certain amount of dramatic irony, which in Chaucer's source would certainly have come from the woman's failure to keep the money, has been sacrificed by our poet to the unity of the tale. For in versions like Boccaccio's where both husband and wife are deceived, ironic implications cross one another's path; from their complication a certain confusion must result, with inevitable weakening of the humorous effect of each bit of irony.[57] Deliberate transformation of his material for concentration of effect would certainly not be surprising on Chaucer's part.[58] But, on the other hand, the loss of a fabliau quite close in plot to the *Shipman's Tale*—as close, let us say, as *Le meunier et les II clers* is to the *Reeve's Tale*—is not impossible at all. We are thus left without any indication as to the nature and extent of Chaucer's contribution to the last scene, in which he has all the dramatic irony center on the husband's attitude:

> "and I foryeve it thee;
> But, by thy lyf, ne be namore so large;
> Keep bet our good, this yeve I thee in charge."[59]

Conclusions in which the deceived ones express their sense of security and proclaim their confidence always contain amusing irony, but the extreme frequency of the motif[60] somewhat weakens the effect for one acquainted with Montaiglon's *Recueil*.

In this dénouement, otherwise so similar to that of the typical fabliau, the husband is neither contemptible nor grotesque. Perhaps the main reason for Chaucer's breaking away from the traditional dupe portrait is his desire to humanize the tale.[61] But there seems to be another reason, too. We

[55] B. 1477–82.

[56] The merchant's request is in itself a good lifelike paragraph. It also creates, at least on a second reading, a little irony: we suspect that the plans have already been made concerning the time and circumstances of the repayment.

[57] Compare the last scenes of the *Mil. T.*

[58] On concentration of effect see chapter vii, on the *Pd. T.*

[59] B. 1620–22.

[60] See *De Guillaume au faucon,* Montaiglon, *Recueil,* II, 92; *Romanz de un chivaler et de sa dame et de un clerk,* II, 215; *Le chevalier a la robe vermeille,* III, 35; *Du prestre ki abevete,* III, 54; *De la dame qui fit III tors entor le moustier,* III, 192; *Des braies au cordelier,* III, 275; *Des tresces,* IV, 67; *De la dame qui fist batre son mari,* IV, 133; *D'Auberée la vielle maquerelle,* V, 1; *De la dame qui fist entendant son mari qu'il sonjoit,* V, 132; *Des III dames qui troverent l'anel au conte,* VI, 1.

[61] As, with different methods, he humanizes most of his tales.

must reread the story with an eye on the *Canterbury Tales* as a whole, remembering that the *Shipman's Tale* was undoubtedly written for the Wife of Bath, to be delivered with an occasional malicious glance at one important, respectable-looking pilgrim sitting "hye on horse." If the cap is to fit at all, the Wife of Bath must be careful to make her merchant keep at least an external appearance of respectability. To portray him as jealous would be to ridicule him too openly. A certain form of dramatic irony is lost by the omission of this almost classical feature of the deception fabliau, but a more than sufficient compensation is offered in the field of dramatic irony itself: the hero's serious, worthy character creates an incongruity as striking as any other, and at bottom much more cruel: an earnest, successful, and satisfied business man—a kind one, too—keeping his look of dignity all through the tale of his misfortunes, and showing the most exquisite tact in his relations with the "cousin" who is deceiving him. No doubt the original plan of the *Canterbury Tales* must have favored the development of this subtly cruel form of dramatic irony at the expense of that which would have raised too loud a laugh.

## The "Friar's Tale"

The widespread story of the devil and his victim was beautifully suited for the Friar's attack upon his fellow-pilgrim. First, the plot involved a good deal of dramatic irony which could be used as a very sharp weapon; and, secondly, there was a chance of making the Summoner supremely odious by presenting a brother of his as worse than the devil himself. Strongly emphasized as it is in the *Friar's Tale,* this contrast involves a sacrifice of realism to the requirements of satire, a rather un-Chaucerian feature which gives a very special, weird, and unreal coloring to the different episodes and their strokes of dramatic irony. This dramatic irony is derived from four motifs: (1) the summoner's eagerness to open friendly relations with his fellow-traveler; (2) his interest in the abode and in the occupations of the devil; (3) his urging him to carry off some victim as soon as he can; and (4) his bringing upon himself the violent curses of the old woman. These four different motifs create dramatic irony through their contrast with one and the same episode, viz., the carrying off of the summoner by the devil. Hence the very striking unity of the tale.

Far from suspecting the possible outcome of the new acquaintanceship, the summoner takes the first step and greets the gay yeoman. Two minutes later, they are "sworne bretheren til they deye," a somewhat conventional expression, to which, however, a second reading adds a touch of grim irony. The same note is felt in the summoner's next question:

> "Brother," quod he, "where is now your dwelling,
> Another day if that I sholde yow seche?"[62]

The "softe speche" of the devil's answer—a first notation of rather sophisticated realism—makes his veiled threat more calmly, more terribly threatening.

> This yeman him answerde in softe speche,
> "Brother," quod he, "fer in the north contree,
> Wher, as I hope, som-tyme I shal thee see,
> Er we departe, I shal thee so wel wisse,
> That of myn hous ne shaltow never misse."[63]

Like Daun Russel's similarly inviting mention of his home in B. 4485–87, these words of the devil are, of course, direct, conscious irony. But in the summoner's failure to perceive this irony, in his easy, unconcerned way of dropping the question as satisfactorily settled, there is almost as much dramatic irony as in any answer he might have given. In the conversation that follows, the likeness of professions and methods causes the future victim to rejoice in the new friendship:

> "Wel be we met, by god and by seint Jame!
> But, leve brother, tel me than thy name, . . . ."[64]

The frank reply of the almost too honest devil introduces the second of our four motifs, the summoner's series of eager questions about hell and its inhabitants. The answers of the fiend—as clear and definite as his companion might wish—culminate in an open threat, which is at the same time a retrospective glance at the dramatic irony of the whole scene:

> But o thing warne I thee, I wol nat jape,
> Thou wolt algates wite how we ben shape;
> Thou shalt her-afterward, my brother dere,
> Com ther thee nedeth nat of me to lere.[65]

Nothing could be clearer, yet here again the summoner seems incredibly deaf, for all he has to answer is that certainly he will never leave his "sworne brother"! He goes farther and introduces our third contrast:

> ". . . . bothe we goon abouten our purchas.
> Tak thou thy part, what that men wol thee yive,
> And I shal myn; . . . ."[66]

The swearing of the angry carter encourages our summoner to stimulate the zeal of his friend in a more definite way.

---

[62] D. 1410–11. [63] D. 1412–16. [64] D. 1443–44.

[65] D. 1513–16. There is a similar allusion in D. 1636–38.

[66] D. 1530–32.

> Herkne, my brother, herkne, by thy feith;
> Herestow nat how that the carter seith?
> Hent it anon, for he hath yeve it thee, . . . .[67]

But the devil has scruples! A poor bailiff, indeed, and one who badly needs the summoner's good example—our fourth motif:

> But for thou canst nat, as in this contree,
> Winne thy cost, tak heer ensample of me.[68]

Extreme cruelty toward the old widow is consistent with the character of the odious extortioner. Still, we half suspect not only that Chaucer exaggerates for the purposes of satire, but that his summoner is going farther than usual in order to stress the contrast of his sensible policy with the foolish niceties of the fiend. He thus falls a prey to the devil, partly through his attempt to secure a victim himself, partly because he tries to give a lesson by his example to one who, by the teacher's undoing, will soon prove that he was in no need of instruction.

For how many of these cases of dramatic irony is Chaucer indebted to his source? That source is lost, and we have no way of determining the literary genre to which it belonged. It may have been a short *exemplum*, a longer version, or a tale transmitted orally; or Chaucer may have run across this widespread story in several different forms.[69] Our third motif is the only point on which there is no doubt: in all analogues worth the name the future victim urges the devil to carry off some person or animal; the episode was undoubtedly present in Chaucer's source. Of the other three motifs, distant suggestions are found here and there among the related versions,[70] but the likeness is never striking enough to suggest close relationship. All we can say is that, whatever Chaucer's source or sources may have offered, the development of these ironical contrasts and their excellent presentation must be largely his own. Indeed, should we for a moment forget the frame of the Canterbury pilgrimage, we would fail to under-

[67] D. 1551–53. [68] D. 1579–80.

[69] On this question, see A. Taylor, "The Devil and the Advocate," *P.M.L.A.*, XXXVI (1921), 35–59, especially p. 59.

[70] Motif one is suggested by the first answer of Rusticus to the devil in the poem of der Stricker (*Der Richter und der Teufel*, found in Karl Goedeke, *Deutsche Dichtung in Mittelalter*, pp. 849–51, or Hagen, *Gesammtabenteuer*, III, 383 ff.). In other versions, on the contrary, the future victim recognizes the devil and tries to avoid him (e.g., the version of Caesarius von Heisterbach, in *Römische Quartalschrift für christliche Alterthumskunde und für Kirchengeschichte, 13e Supplementheft* [Rome, 1901]). Motif two is suggested (very vaguely) in lines 45 ff. of the poem of der Stricker, and motif four in *Der Advocat und der Rothmantel* of Langbein, summarized by Taylor, *op. cit.*, pp. 53–55, and in a version taken down in Hesse (see Taylor, *op. cit.*, pp. 43–44).

stand the main function of the irony of Chaucer's tale as a weapon in the Friar's hands. And a very effective weapon it is! To our intense dislike of the extortioner in the tale (our dislike as roused by other means), it adds darker and more complex feelings: a vague fear and horror of a monster mocked and perhaps even marked out by Fate, to which horror a grim and harsh smile of derision is added, with perhaps a merciless gratification of both our cruelty and our sense of humor. But this form of grim humor itself is valuable mainly as one of the Friar's offensive arms, i.e., in the pilgrimage setting created by Chaucer.

## The "Summoner's Tale"

In *Li dis de la vescie a prestre,*[71] the French trouvère Jakes de Baisiu tells us a story very similar to the *Summoner's Tale*: A sick man is visited by two grasping friars, who urge him to make a gift to their convent. Wanting to punish them for their hypocrisy and avarice, he promises a rich present, then disappoints the friars by a mock gift.

Deceived expectations easily give rise to dramatic irony, especially in the hands of French trouvères, who do not often overlook the cruel side of a joke. The rimers rarely comment on such irony, but make their heroes bring it out by words or deeds: in this particular case, by the humorously depicted banquet in which the whole convent indulges to celebrate the coming gift,[72] then by the gathering of sheriffs and mayor for the ceremony of the donation.[73] To Jakes de Baisiu, these ironic circumstances, carefully recapitulated in the concluding lines,[74] seem to have been the main point in the tale.

Not so with Chaucer. No doubt the irony of the friar's hopes was present in the very plot as supplied by the source of the *Summoner's Tale.*[75] But Chaucer's interest was not so much in the story itself as in a striking portrait of a hypocritical and covetous friar, the only suitable form for the Summoner's retort to the story of the devil and his victim. Yet it happens that the characterization features on which the emphasis had to be laid greatly strengthen the irony inherent in the plot: the more intense the friar's yearning for gold, the stronger the contrast of his efforts and hopes with their ridiculous outcome. This effect of vivid character drawing on dramatic irony admirably served the teller's purposes of ridiculing his hero,

[71] Montaiglon, *Recueil,* III, 106 ff., and *Or. and An.,* pp. 137–44.

[72] Ll. 162–81. [73] Ll. 239–41. [74] Ll. 311–17.

[75] How close this source may have been to our fabliau, it is difficult to say. It may be worth noting that Jakes de Baisiu locates his convent in Antwerp. A fabliau of the North had especially good chances of reaching our poet, either in England or in the course of one of his many journeys on the Continent.

and for this reason must have been very welcome to Chaucer. Indeed, the choice of the theme must have been determined by the poet's full appreciation of such possibilities.

To the irony inherent in the plot Chaucer's tale adds that of the friar's sermon against anger.[76] The preaching is hardly over when the sick man waxes "wel ny wood for ire,"[77] and the preacher himself starts up "as doth a wood leoun."[78] This amusing touch is probably our poet's own contribution. Not only is the whole sermon taken from *Jerome against Jovinian* and Seneca[79]—both more familiar to Chaucer than to French trouvères—but such irony resting exclusively on character reactions is hardly likely to have been suggested by any fabliau.

One of the illustrations of wrath in the friar's sermon, the crime of Cambyses,[80] is taken from Seneca, who with characteristic definiteness points out the tragic irony of his story: "*Videbimus quomodo se pater gerere debuerit stans super cadaver fili sui caedemque illam, cuius et testis fuerat et causa.*" In the friar's perfunctory and disconnected sermon, similar words would have constituted no worse a digression than the remark on the wisdom of singing *Placebo* to the exalted ones.[81] But they might have raised the interest of Chaucer's readers more than was desirable, diverting their attention from the hypocritical preacher seated on his bench to the dramatic irony at work at the Persian court of King Cambyses. Chaucer preferred to abstain, showing thereby that moderation and that sureness of judgment which we shall note again and again in chapter ix of this study.

## The "Merchant's Tale"

For variety and life within his "marriage group" Chaucer was relying on the clash of opposite opinions concerning wedlock. One especially classical theory, so to speak, could by no means be omitted—the cynical view of women and married life, a literary convention all through the Middle Ages. And the greater the bitterness of this attack the better for the marriage group as a whole.

Was dramatic irony to be used in such a tale? Almost inevitably, for Chaucer was very familiar both with the fabliau literature and with Deschamps' *Miroir de mariage*.[82] To the former he would naturally resort

---

[76] He preaches against another vice of his, viz., gluttony, but no doubt perceives the irony.

[77] D. 2121.

[78] D. 2152–55. See also D. 2158–61, 2166–68.

[79] See Skeat's *Complete Works of Chaucer,* V, 338; F. Tupper, *Mod. Lang. Notes,* XXX (1915), 8–9.

[80] D. 2043–73.

[81] D. 2074–78.

[82] *Le miroir de mariage, Œuvres complètes de Eustache Deschamps,* Vol. IX, Société des Anciens Textes Français (Paris, 1894).

for the "woman's wiles" plot that he needed, and the second, a monument of misogyny previously drawn upon in the "marriage group,"[83] would inevitably be brought back to his memory by the very purpose of the tale. From both sides, incitements to make use of dramatic irony were almost sure to come. First, from the fabliaux: this point needs no development, for we know that a dupe story, well told or not, in French or Italian garb, always offers at least chances for dramatic irony, often of the very inviting kind. The part played by the *Miroir* is less obvious. Indeed, that any encouragement to the use of dramatic irony may have come from a poem entirely destitute of such irony[84] sounds somewhat paradoxical at first. We need a summary of the *Miroir*:

Franc Vouloir is urged to marry by his false friends Désir, Folie, Servitude, and Fantaisie. Wavering between fears and hopes, he decides to submit the whole matter to his faithful friend Répertoire de Science, who answers with a violent disquisition against women, and an advocacy of spiritual marriage. The false friends repeat some of their former arguments in rebuttal. In the course of the discussion the poem breaks off abruptly.

For the purposes of the present study, the most interesting passage in the *Miroir* is chapter xi, more exactly lines 722–73, where Franc Vouloir momentarily indulges in visions of happiness with an ideal wife:

"Mais avoir vueil femme benigne ...
Juene et chaste de bouche et mains
Saige et gente, et qui ait du mains
De .XV., .XVI. ou a vint ans, ...
Plus l'ameray que riens mortele,
En joie fineray mon temps,
Je n'aray noise ne contemps,
Je seray gaiz et envoisés,
Je seray tousjours bien aisés
Et hors de ces aultres perils
De foles femmes qui sont vils ...
Je viveray selon la loy ...
Et mes enfens qui demourront
Moy leur pere ramenbreront ...
Et croy que ce sera le mieulx."

Keeping in mind that several echoes of this passage are found in January's own anticipations of "paradies,"[85] one wonders whether the contrast of

[83] See J. L. Lowes, "Chaucer and the *Miroir de mariage*," *Mod. Phil.*, VIII (1910–11), 165–86 and 305–34, especially pp. 305–21, on numerous and striking echoes of the *Miroir* in the *W.B.P.*

[84] Except for the ordinary dupe irony of the fabliaux in stories given as examples, e.g., in chapter xxxviii.

[85] See Lowes, *op. cit.*, especially pp. 173–74.

Franc Vouloir's hopeful mood with the vivid, realistic picture that follows in the answer of Répertoire de Science was not enough in itself to suggest to a greater artist—already a past master in the handling of irony—the possibility of a more dramatic contrast: similar dreams against the dreamer's own future experiences? In any case, Chaucer's familiarity with the allegorical counselors of the *Miroir* must have had something to do with the unusual importance (if not with the very conception) of the deliberation scenes in the *Merchant's Tale,*[86] which scenes, in Chaucer's hands, proved such marvelous opportunities for dramatic irony. Thus the use of the device in this attack upon women and marriage was suggested by both the fabliaux and the *Miroir.* Chaucer's merit is not in having followed the suggestion but in the sureness of insight with which he recognized a sustained use of dramatic irony as the most powerful weapon for the attack he was planning, in the boldness with which he struck in the first pages blows of maximum severity, and in the creative vigor which allowed him to keep up through the twelve hundred lines of his tale this tense feeling of fierce irony.

Let us study the details.

The age of January has puzzled many critics as an unjustified addition to the pear tree story. Whatever Chaucer's main reason for this may have been, the change greatly heightens the effect of dramatic irony. It weakens the attack on women's depravity and helps to place the main emphasis on men's incurable folly, i.e., on the character of January, around whom centers all the irony of the tale. To this irony it imparts a distinctly tragic coloring: the mistake of a younger man would leave chances of compensation in the future, but the failure of old January is the shattering of his last hope—perhaps the one hope of his epicurean life!

As usual with Chaucer's careful calculation of ironical effects we are allowed to anticipate the hero's coming troubles. Definite prophecies will come in time,[87] but as early as E. 1253 and 1266 (ll. 9 and 22 of the tale) the tone of sarcasm is itself more than a hint. Hence the dramatic irony of January's very first words:

> "Non other lyf," seyde he, "is worth a bene;
> For wedlock is so esy and so clene,
> That in this world it is a paradys."[88]

---

[86] On the influence of Melibeus on that part of the *Mch. T.* plot, see J. S. P. Tatlock, *Development and Chronology* (Ch. Soc., 1907), pp. 215–16, and J. Lowes, *op. cit.,* note 5 to p. 185 (continued on p. 305).

[87] E. 1781–82:

> But ther I lete him [Damian] wepe y-nough and pleyne,
> Til fresshe May wol rewen on his peyne.

[88] E. 1263–65.

These and similar words can only too easily be paralleled in the speeches of Deschamps' four counselors:

> "Mariage est souverain bien
> Et sur tous la plus belle vie,"[89]

but such resemblances should not be given too much importance. As noted before, the soliloquy where Franc Vouloir expresses his hopes is infinitely more likely to have encouraged Chaucer to lay stress on the illusions of January.

In the next one hundred and twenty-five lines—the Merchant's parenthesis on the evils of married life—there could not be any dramatic irony, either at the expense of the teller, whose ironical thrusts are all intentional, or at that of the characters in his tale, since the comment is interrupting all action.[90] The passage, however, interests us here because of its effect on the strokes of dramatic irony that follow: the Merchant's satire not only helps to build up the atmosphere of extreme bitterness that will give the irony of action its unique character, but also allows us to anticipate January's coming troubles more definitely than we could if we were less keenly aware of the teller's real feelings about married life.[91]

---

[89] Ll. 9006–7.

[90] It must be noted, however, that the smooth, elusive transition by which the Merchant brings us back from his parenthesis to the story proper,

> For which this Januarie, of whom I tolde,
> Considered hath . . . .
>
> —E. 1393–94

half suggests that at least the words immediately preceding should be considered not only as the teller's own ironical blow, but at the same time as his phrasing of January's thought:

> They been so knit, ther may noon harm bityde;
> And namely, up-on the wyves syde.
>
> —E. 1391–92

Attributed to January, the words would, indeed, contain dramatic irony: somewhere in the back of his mind there may be a feeling that some harm might come because his virtue cannot be trusted completely!

Incidentally, the same general remarks—ironical here, too—on the advantages of married life close with exactly the same transition in *Les états du siècle* (Montaiglon, *Recueil,* II, 264):

> S'elle luy voit le cuer mary,
> Trés doucement le reconforte.
> Assés d'autre prouffit luy porte.
> *Pour ce* tantoust se maria
> Pour le grant aise qu'il y a.

[91] On a second reading, we even notice, among the teller's blows of direct irony, several veiled allusions to the events in the second half of the tale, which allusions

January is considering all sides of the question. For his objections against a widow we have several explanations: Chaucer takes hints certainly from Albertanus[92] and very probably from the *Miroir*,[93] and he evidently wishes to make his Merchant strike a blow at the Wife of Bath.[94] But the main reason why he insists on the advantages of choosing a young wife is no doubt the piteous irony of January's precautions in contrast with

---

naturally help to keep up even clearer anticipations than were possible on the first reading. When the solidity of wedlock is compared to the "brotelnesse" of bachelors' love affairs, we think of January's coming misfortunes in married life, and of the success of Damian, a bachelor. The advisability of working after a "wyves reed" reminds us of January following May's advice on the fatal day when he takes her to the garden. Finally, the comparison of those irregular ways of unmarried men with the life "of a brid or of a beste" calls to mind the future scene in the tree.

Like so many other parts of the Merchant's ironical praise of marriage, this mention of a bird appears to have been suggested by the *Miroir:*

> "Suis plus frans que l'oisel du raim
> Qui puet ou il lui plaist voler."
>
> —Ll. 528–29

Professor J. L. Lowes (*op. cit.*, pp. 180–81) draws attention to the *Miroir* (ll. 2943–48) as suggesting a possible association of ideas for the fusion of the *Miroir* with the pear tree story (a view strongly supported by the fact that Chaucer, in E. 2268–75, almost certainly used the lines immediately following on *Miroir* l. 2948). The two lines quoted above may have helped the same association. A third passage had, I believe, a better chance. It is the opening of chapter vi:

> "*Thobie perdit sa lueur*
> *Mais sa femme lui fut aidable,*
> Treshumble, douce et charitable,
> Et a lui garder entendi
> *Tant que Dieux clarté lui rendi; ...*"

We must remember that the preceding chapter was extensively used by Chaucer, and also that the part played in the *Mch. T.* by Proserpine and Pluto is played by God and St. Peter in several analogues, among others the Italian *Novellino.* On this same question of the association of ideas that brought the pear tree story, see Professor Tatlock's suggestion, *Angl.*, XXXVII (1913), 102–3.

To close our list of the Merchant's veiled allusions to the fabliau half of the tale, we must mention here a line of comment that occurs a little later in the course of the narrative itself: when January chooses his bride "of his owene auctoritee" (E. 1598), the Merchant's explanation, "for love is blind al day, and may nat see," immediately connects in our minds January's first form of blindness with another form that awaits him, a tragically ironical coincidence. The common saying that love is blind probably suggested the phrase. Cf., in the *Kn. T.*, A. 1796–97 and 1965.

92 See E. Koeppel, "Chaucer und Albertanus Brixiensis," *Archiv.*, LXXXVI (1891), 29–46.

93 Ll. 726–27, 1074–76.

94 As is made clear especially in E. 1428.

the cynicism and impudence of that "young thing" chosen for her innocence. Two lines deserve special attention:

> "But certeynly, a yong thing may men gye,
> Right as men may warm wex with handes plye."[95]

The best parallel is in the *Miroir,* just three lines after the passage on the age of the ideal wife:

> Et doulce comme columbelle,
> Obeissant a moy en tout,[96]

but I have not found anywhere a mention of wax which could have suggested either the comparison in the lines quoted above or the second appearance of warm wax in the tale, when it is used by May herself for counterfeiting the key in order to admit her lover into the garden.[97] All we could hope to find would of course be a parallel for one of the two passages, the use of warm wax in the other remaining in any case one of Chaucer's most subtle twists of dramatic irony: no simple, well-balanced contrast of one thing with the reverse of it,[98] but a lighter, defter touch, more seemingly innocent, yet striking enough to wake us up violently by establishing a relation startling almost in proportion to its being illogical—a malign, whimsical imp must be creating incongruities, following methods that escape us. For this type of dramatic irony neither the finest fabliaux nor the rest of Chaucer's probable or possible reading offers the slightest parallel.

Our hero knows what he is about:

> "I dote nat, I woot the cause why
> Men sholde wedde, and forthermore wot I,
> Ther speketh many a man of mariage,
> That woot na-more of it than woot my page."[99]

"Not more than my page" may have been a current expression, but even so an ironical intention almost certainly dictated its choice:[100] one of

[95] E. 1429–30.

[96] Ll. 730–31.

[97] E. 2116–17. In the French farce *De Pernet qui va au vin* and in its derivative, Heywood's *Johan Johan the husbande,* a husband is set to chafing wax by lovers who want him out of the way. The motif may have been a familiar feature of deception plots. But it is not the dupe who chafes wax in the *Mch. T.,* and this essential difference makes a connection appear rather improbable. On this farce, see Karl Young, "The Influence of the French Farce upon the Plays of John Heywood," *Mod. Phil.,* II (1904), 97–124, especially 101–6.

[98] E.g., of January's expectation to find a young girl like wax, and the fact that he himself would turn wax in her hands.

[99] E. 1441–44.

[100] Damian, we must admit, is no longer a page, but already a squire. Also the rime "page / mariage" is a rather easy one.

January's retinue, indeed, will soon enough show familiarity with certain possibilities of married life.

The knight begins to look around. He dismisses from his thought those young women that are rich but have "badde name," preferring the guaranty of "sadnesse." For the chief factor of his coming happiness is to be that secure feeling that he will

> han hire al,
> That no wight of his blisse parten shal.[101]

The next stroke, January's fear of losing his chance of eternal bliss in his enjoyment of a terrestrial paradise, is one of almost unbearable cruelty. The thread of associations that suggested it to Chaucer does not seem to be entirely hidden from us. To retrace it, we must, I believe, work backward, starting with the bitter retort of Justinus:

> "Dispeire yow noght, but have in your memorie,
> Paraunter she may be your purgatorie,"[102]

which retort must take us for a moment away from dramatic irony. The Merchant, we have already observed, is keeping in mind the Wife of Bath and her theory of married life, and gradually leading up to a direct attack soon to be put in the mouth of Justinus.[103] An excellent chance for a little side-blow presents itself here: by the picturesque character of her language the Wife had prepared the way for those who would choose to retort indirectly,[104] for any comparison of a woman with either purgatory or a whip was sure to make the pilgrims turn and smile. A desire to achieve this effect of excellent comedy almost certainly dictated to Chaucer the direct irony of Justinus' remark, which in its turn called for the speech that it

---

[101] E. 1629–30.

[102] E. 1669–70.

[103] E. 1684–87. On that direct attack, see G. L. Kittredge, "Chaucer's Discussion of Marriage," *Mod. Phil.,* IX (1912), 435–67. I find a very similar violation of dramatic propriety in the *Roman de la Rose,* where Genius, in his speech delivered in the name of Nature, alludes to the *Roman:*

> "Les vices conter vous voldroie
> Mes d'outrage m'entremetroie;
> Asses briefment les vous expose
> Li jolis Romant de la Rose."
> —Marteau ed., ll. 20591 ff.

("Asses briefment" is a medieval computation of time!)

[104] Cf. the whole *W.B.P.* to E. 1423–28, 1684–87; D. 175, 489–90 to E. 1637–73; D. 688–92, 706 to the *Cl. T.;* D. 788–828 and the whole *W.B.T.,* to F. 742–43, E. 1170–1212, and even, in the *Parson's Tale,* I, 925–27 (though this is a translation and the irony is probably accidental).

was to refute, i.e., for those lamentably ridiculous reflections of poor January on the "parfit felicitee" that is in marriage and his fear of not having his due earthly share of "tribulacioun and greet penaunce." We have thus dramatic irony eagerly seized by Chaucer and ruthlessly developed in a passage of eighteen lines,[105] but rather accidentally suggested to him by his attention to the frame of the *Canterbury Tales,* not the Merchant's story.[106]

One line of the speech of January deserves special attention:

> "For though he kepe him fro the sinnes sevene,
> And eek from every branche of thilke tree . . . ."[107]

This tree with its branches of sin, trite as the metaphor may be, makes us think of another tree, somehow connected with sin too, and from which January will keep or, rather, be kept.[108] As in the case of "warm wex," we are perplexed by the very absence of any logical connection. It seems as if some malign power were taking delight in making the mind of old helpless January play with those very things—a tree, warm wax—that are to cause the final ruin of his hopes. Or does his very mention of those objects call fate upon him?

When the priest who unites the couple makes "al siker y-nogh with holinesse,"[109] the main dramatic irony is not at his expense, for he remains a secondary figure, but at the expense of old January, who, we know, is following the ritual with entire faith in its efficacy. As part of this service, the allusion to Rebecca should perhaps be noted. Previously she had been mentioned by the Merchant as one of the women whose counsels had proved good.[110] Into each of the two passages her name may be brought accidentally, first in the series of examples copied straight from *Melibeus,* then as part of the marriage service. And yet the recurrence is striking and at

---

[105] E. 1637–54.

[106] I do not feel any intention of recalling this irony in E. 1265, 1332, and 1822, where the word "paradise" means only "bliss," and passes almost unnoticed.

[107] E. 1640–41.

[108] The relative frequency of the mentions of trees in the early part of the tale suggests intentional dramatic irony. In E. 1461–66, January compares himself first with a tree in blossom, then with a laurel "alwey grene." Trees are supposed to wear more blossoms the year before they die, and a laurel green throughout the year is said not to be in the best of condition. As possible suggestions for the comparison, see *Miroir,* ll. 117–25 and 200–203.

[109] E. 1708. The word "holinesse" here means religion (see J. S. P. Tatlock, *Studies in Philology,* XVIII [1921], pp. 422–25). On this marriage service and its ironical implications, see also J. S. P. Tatlock, "The Marriage Service in the *Merchant's Tale,*" *Mod. Lang. Notes,* XXXII (1917), 373–74.

[110] E. 1362–65.

least suggests an ironical intention: did not Rebecca, too, resort to wiles to deceive a weak-sighted old husband?[111]

Very different is the effect reached through emphasis on the joy of the newly wedded January: the ironical intention here seems, by contrast, almost too clear, the method almost too simple. There is more refined and subtle cruelty in the stress laid on his scruples and delicate feelings toward May,[112] a creature almost too tender, too spotless and pure to belong here in this rough world of ours.

The fulfillment of January's hopes brings us to the last part of the tale, the pear tree story. Professor Varnhagen[113] offers good reasons for considering the version of the Italian *Novellino*[114] as Chaucer's source, though we cannot be sure that it was the direct source: a French fabliau[115]

---

[111] As part of the same service, the name of Sarra is coupled with that of Rebekke. I strongly suspect this emphasis on the marriage ritual to have been suggested by *Miroir,* ll. 275 ff.:

> Celle Saire que nous disons
> Fu si loyal qu'es benissons
> Est nommée et es espousailles.

The passage occurs just twenty-three lines below "Thobie perdit sa lueur," on which see p. 49, note 91, above.

[112] E. 1755–61, 1828 ff.

[113] "Zu Chaucers Erzählung des Kaufmanns," *Angl.,* Bd. VII (1884), Anz. 155–65.

[114] Printed by G. Papanti, *Catalogo dei novellieri italiani in prosa* (Livorno, 1871), Vol. I, Appendix, pp. xliii f.; by G. Biagi, *Le novelle antiche* (Firenze, 1880), No. 155, p. 199; and by Holthausen, *Engl. Stud.,* XLIII (1910), 168–69.

[115] The story was very popular, and Caxton tells us plainly that he translates his *Blynd Man and his Wyf* (*Or. and An.,* pp. 181–82) from the French. Two other facts suggest the loss of a French version of a story which could not be Chaucer's source, but is close enough to it to be of a certain interest here: from a tree into which he has climbed a husband sees his wife with her lover, but he accepts the tree as enchanted and as responsible for an optical illusion (see the Arabian version in *Or. and An.,* pp. 353–55). (*a*) In the fabliau *Du prestre ki abevete* (Montaiglon, *Recueil,* III, 54), a hole in a door plays exactly the same part as the supposedly enchanted pear tree. A connection is unquestionable, and the rather prosaic hole could hardly be the more primitive element. (*b*) The current French expression *"faire monter quelqu'un à l'arbre"* (jestingly make him believe something rather absurd and even act on the false information) seems likely to have had its origin in a version in which the husband was made to climb the tree. Professor A. M. Espinosa tells me that the story of the enchanted tree as we know it from the Arabian version is still current in Spanish folklore, that the tree is a fig tree, and that allusions to fig trees occur in stories of deception. This makes a connection of the French expression with a similar story appear rather probable. I have unfortunately not succeeded in tracing the phrase back to Old French. It may have originated with our theme though rather recently, perhaps with some of the French works based on *Decam.,* VII, 9 (La Fontaine's *Les trois commères,* or any of the many vaudevilles and comedies listed by A. C. Lee, *op. cit.,* p. 240), which works might then represent the first appearance of the story in French literature.

may have served as a link between the Italian and the English, a possibility that we shall have to keep in mind.

The knight's innocent surprise, his sympathetic interest in Damian, whom we know to be sick for love of May, are not paralleled in the rather brief *Novellino.* They strikingly recall the questions of the carpenter about "hende Nicholas" in the *Miller's Tale*[116] and are as typically fabliau as possible:

> "He is a gentil squyer, by my trouthe!
> If that he deyde, it were harm and routhe."[117]

He is, indeed, in danger, as lovers were in the Middle Ages, but January must not worry: like Alison in the *Miller's Tale,* May will see to it that the young man does not die. January's praise of Damian as discreet, "secree," masculine, and "servisable,"[118] the very traits that enable the lover to injure him, are on a higher level of humor. The irony of the scene culminates when January sends May to visit Damian and urges her to be kind to him.[119] This amusing stroke—for this is rather comedy—I believe to be Chaucer's entirely. It is not suggested in the Italian, and, even if Chaucer used some lost fabliau, he is not likely to have found there such a circumstantial account of the way the lovers came together. A trouvère was infinitely more likely to go straight to the pear tree episode. As suggested by Professor Tatlock,[120] Chaucer's "source" here may very well have been one of his own earlier creations, the scene where his Pandarus sends Criseyde to the bedside of lovesick Troilus.[121] We would then have an entirely original motif transferred from one poem of Chaucer into another, the contrast of the scene formerly narrated with the situation in the new tale being perceived by the poet as an opportunity for dramatic irony in spite of all the differences of setting and tone.[122]

---

[116] A. 3423 ff. On the many points of contact between the *Mil. T.* and the *Mch. T.*, see note 43, p. 37, above. [117] E. 1907–8. [118] E. 1909–12. [119] E. 1920–28.

[120] *Development and Chronology,* p. 216, note 2.

[121] Also E. 1967 ff. suggest a recently renewed contact with *Tr. and Cr.*

[122] The use in E. 1986 of Chaucer's favorite line "Lo, pitee renneth sone in gentil herte" (the source of which is of course well known: *Divina Commedia,* Inferno, V, 100), may have been suggested by the irony of *Miroir,* ll. 2922 ff.:

> Juvenaulx les mariez tance
> Et content qu'il n'est femme chaste,
> S'on la poursuit et s'on la haste;
> *Que la nature est enclinable*
> *D'estre a tout homme secourable,*
> Et que c'est ly mendre pechiez.

Cf. also E. 1987 ff., and notice the proximity of the passage just quoted to lines 2943 ff. and 2949 ff., of which Professor Lowes has pointed out the significance.

Old January's unwelcome manifestations of love,[123] when May has just read Damian's letter and is "studying" how she may fulfill the young man's desire, have a hard ironical flavor. She "studies" a long time in vain, then January himself goes halfway to meet her wishes by having a garden planted and walled. Writing a similar story, a trouvère would simply have informed his readers of the existence of the garden needed as a setting. That the future dupe should have planned it himself adds a secondary touch of cruel dramatic irony for the invention of which we can almost safely credit our poet's own imagination.

As the tale proceeds, the mood of dramatic irony is kept up by the recurrence of those details mentioned above in connection with January's anticipations: May counterfeits the key with warm wax, and it is on her instigation—a woman's advice—that January decides to go to the garden on the fatal day. A particular line in his love song, largely taken from the Song of Solomon, must have been welcome to Chaucer for the dramatic irony which it creates in the new setting:

> "No spot of thee ne knew I al myn lyf."[124]

The ironical intention is even clearer when January, having carefully shut the wicket of the garden into which Damian has preceded him, says in the very next line:

> "Now wyf, . . . . heer nis but thou and I."[125]

This introduces a speech of humble prayer, an elaborate encouragement to remain a faithful wife.[126] While January speaks, May is making signs to Damian.

The dramatic irony of the last scenes comes nearer to the typical irony of the fabliaux, and it is difficult to guess what Chaucer may have found in his source if that source was not our *Novellino*. If it was, Chaucer developed a few suggestions in his usual way. When the Italian wife says that she will climb the tree to get some pears, her husband answers, *"chiama chi ti ne colga,"* and the reader, of course, thinks of the lover who is already in the tree. Chaucer has made this irony not only more definite, but also lamentably pathetic, seizing the opportunity to make the poor blind man express his helpless devotion to young May:

> "Allas!" quod he, "that I ne had heer a knave
> That coude climbe; allas! allas!" quod he,
> "That I am blind."[127]

---

[123] E. 1957 ff.

[124] E. 2146. Cf. the Song of Solomon, iv. 7: "Thou art all fair, O my love; there is no spot in thee."

[125] E. 2160; notice the same irony in E. 2136.

[126] E. 2168 ff.

[127] E. 2338–40.

The same tone is preserved when January helps May into the tree, a cruel stroke unparalleled in other versions but very probably suggested by a version close to the *Novellino,* if not by the *Novellino* itself: *"e il marito abraccia il pedale del pero, prechè non v'andasse persona dietro le."* For the sake of such harsh ironical contrasts the tellers (Italian or French) occasionally accepted rather palpable exaggerations. Chaucer has kept this one, possibly for its dramatic irony, but chiefly, I should suspect, because he had thought of enlarging upon it by making the suggestion of holding the tree trunk come from May,[128] thus giving his Merchant an additional chance to portray women as almost repulsively cynical.

Whatever Chaucer's source may have been, the unbearable cruelty of E. 2357–60 is almost certainly our poet's contribution. Who else, in the course of the ribald tale, would have devoted four long lines to the psychology of the victim?

> And whan that he hadde caught his sighte agayn,
> Ne was ther never man of thing so fayn.
> But on his wyf his thoght was evermo;
> Up to the tree he caste his eyen two . . . .

The *Novellino* gives us here exactly the dry and objective account we would expect: *"ora vidde lume et guatò in sùe, e vidde quello che la donna faciea."*

For a superficial reader, the tale ends in the classical manner of the "women's wiles" fabliaux, i.e., by a charitable and successful lulling into sleep of the one spark of clearsightedness betrayed by the dupe in the course of the tale:

> This Januarie, who is glad but he?[129]

But the impression is not that of comedy. In the last few pages, what little sympathy the reader can feel has been enlisted on the side of January, so that all the bitterness and resentment stirred up against women in the first part of the tale come back to us and make that last touch of irony almost as different in feeling from the usual dénouement of a fabliau as the *Merchant's Tale* on the whole differs from *La borgoise d'Orliens* or *Des tresces.*

In several respects the dramatic irony of the *Merchant's Tale* is unique in Chaucer's works. First of all, and as far as such things can be measured, the ironies of life seem to play here an even larger part than, let us say, in the *Reeve's* or the *Pardoner's Tales.* A larger part, and also a more essential one, for that mood of intense bitterness that makes the *Merchant's Tale*

---

128 E. 2341 ff.

129 E. 2412. On the frequency of this motif see p. 41, note 60, above.

stand apart in the Canterbury collection is due primarily to Chaucer's handling of the irony of action. His success in using the device with such effectiveness is due largely to the intensity and subtlety of the individual strokes, but even more to their number, to that inexhaustible power of invention which allowed Chaucer to keep up through his long tale the mood of fierce irony so boldly pitched at its highest point in the opening pages—another feature unparalleled in the other works. And, finally, though well-presented dramatic irony always implies appreciation by the narrator, that of the Merchant's is unique in its continual and exceptionally definite suggestion of the teller's resentful and embittered state.

## IV. THE *WIFE OF BATH'S TALE*

We possess three Middle English analogues to the *Wife of Bath's Tale:* Gower's *Tale of Knight Florent,*[1] a romance entitled *The Wedding of Sir Gawain and Dame Ragnel,*[2] and a ballad, *The Marriage of Sir Gawaine.*[3] Wherever those three versions agree with the *Wife of Bath's Tale* we can assume that they would have agreed with Chaucer's source, too. But there are divergences that raise unsolvable questions concerning several features of that source.[4] Three instances of dramatic irony will be considered.

1. A first ironical contrast results from the nature of the knight's original crime, the rape of a maid. We imagine him standing amid the "clamour" raised by this "oppressioun," and we smile thinking of the approaching change—from sheer violence to such perfect meekness—in his attitude toward women. Did Chaucer find in his source this introductory episode which has no parallel in the other extant versions?[5] Against this view of Mr. Maynadier, Mr. W. W. Greg has presented stronger arguments than could be supplied by considerations of dramatic irony.[6] Still it may be worth adding that the literary genre to which lost analogues of the *Wife of Bath's Tale* would probably have belonged, i.e., the folk tale, contains only dramatic irony of a much simpler and more obvious kind than the subtle touch just noted. Furthermore, dramatic irony in the folk tales is used

---

[1] *Or. and An.,* pp. 483 ff.

[2] The outline of this romance, given by Professor Child in *English and Scottish Ballads,* is reprinted in *Or. and An.,* pp. 498 ff.

[3] Printed in *Or. and An.,* pp. 502 ff. The other so-called analogues have the transformation motif without the question motif, and can be left out of consideration here. See G. Maynadier, *"The Wife of Bath's Tale"; Its Sources and Analogues* (London, 1901), and H. Kern, "De Bronnen van *The Wife of Bath's Tale* en daarmede verwante vertellingen," *Verslagen der Kon. Akad. van Wetenschap, Afd. Letterkunde,* 4[de] Reeks, 9, 3.

[4] Chaucer may not have known any version which we do not possess. Yet some of the features peculiar to the *W.B.T.* have a certain flavor of early tradition: (*a*) the fairy nature of the lady (elsewhere, she is a damsel bewitched by her stepmother); (*b*) the twenty-four damsels who dance on the green and then suddenly vanish (this is faerie for faerie's sake); (*c*) the more logical sequence of events. In the three analogues, the lady can regain her true form only by obtaining sovereignty over a peerless knight. Yet she does regain it (at least temporarily) before she even offers the choice that will give her sovereignty. On this point, see W. W. Greg's review of the book of Maynadier, *Mod. Lang. Quar.,* V, 76–79.

[5] Gower's hero has killed a man; in the romance, Arthur has shot a hart; in the ballad, the passage happens to be missing, but the rest of the poem shows no special closeness to Chaucer.

[6] W. W. Greg, *op. cit.,* pp. 78–79.

almost exclusively to bring out the central feature of a narrative; it is very rarely spent on such secondary episodes as our introduction to the tale of the Wife of Bath.[7] For these reasons, even disregarding for a while the arguments of Mr. Greg, the probability seems strong that Chaucer himself added the rape episode for the sake of its humorous effect.

2. The feeling of relief, the perfect assurance, with which the knight accepts and delivers the "pistel . . . . rouned in his ere" by the old hag creates an irony of light and graceful character:

> This knight ne stood nat stille as doth a best,
> But to his questioun anon answerde
> *With manly voys,* that al the court it herde.[8]

To what extent can this stroke be credited to Chaucer? His source no doubt supplied him with the basic ironical contrast: a hero is led to state a truth that will soon be illustrated at his own expense.[9] But what sharpens this irony in the *Wife of Bath's Tale* is the calculated antithesis of the knight's bearing while pronouncing the words with the submissiveness to which the truth of the said words will soon enough reduce him. That Chaucer should be indebted to any lost version of the story for this touch of characterization seems hardly imaginable. On the other hand, the dramatic irony of the stroke owes much of its strength to a feature that may not be Chaucer's contribution to the plot, the unnamed boon motif. In our three analogues, the hag makes her conditions plain at the very start, so that the knight who delivers the answer at least knows of the future marriage. The fact that, in the *Wife of Bath's Tale,* the hero is so far from suspecting the nature of the coming request obviously enhances the humorous irony of his attitude. Did Chaucer introduce the unnamed boon motif with that end in view? No doubt he had met it in many folk tales, and a free handling of his source for the sake of dramatic irony would not surprise us in the least. But the very frequency of the motif opens another possibility: Chaucer may very well have found it already combined with the question story known to Gower.[10]

---

[7] A typical example of folk-tale dramatic irony occurs in Grimm's *Haenzel und Gretel,* when the old sorceress prepares to burn little Gretel in the oven in which she herself is finally thrown.

[8] D. 1034–36.

[9] Little irony results from this contrast in Gower's version, where the hag has made her request plain from the beginning, and Knight Florent, hoping to save his life without having to marry her, tries all other answers before making use of hers. In the romance and in the ballad the question-answerer and the man who is to marry the lady are two different characters.

[10] The perfect appropriateness of the tale to the Wife of Bath is no reason for attributing anything of its plot to Chaucer's invention, for all the elements that make for that fitness are contained in earlier English versions.

3. Like any other folk-tale transformation, that of the ugly old hag into a beautiful young woman could hardly go without dramatic irony; the suddenness and completeness of such metamorphoses are the very essence of this and similar folk tales, and the contrast of expectations and realization accordingly runs no risk of being overlooked.[11] The analogues we possess elaborately stress the feelings of bridegroom or assembly before the transformation. Chaucer's superiority is one of expression: in little space, by a happier choice of details, he creates a situation much tenser and more interesting:

> . . . . prively he wedded hir on a morwe,
> And al day after hidde him as an oule.[12]
>
> He walweth, and he turneth to and fro.
> His olde wyf lay smylinge evermo, . . . .[13]
>
> For Ioye he hente hir in his armes two,
> His herte bathed in a bath of blisse; . . . .[14]

To sum up, with the humor and lightness that so perfectly fit this graceful tale, Chaucer has brought out three different points of dramatic irony. The first of these seems to be his contribution entirely, the second he developed from his source, and the third he simply took over as part of the story.

---

[11] The ballad offers here a touch of dramatic irony not found elsewhere. In stanza 36, when Sir Kay expresses his disgust, Sir Gawaine requires him to hold his peace, apparently not knowing that he will have to marry the loathsome hag himself. As important fragments of this ballad are lost, the connections are not perfectly clear.

[12] D. 1080–81. [13] D. 1085–86. [14] D. 1252–53.

## V. THE *FRANKLIN'S TALE*

The Breton origin of the *Franklin's Tale*[1] has been satisfactorily classed as one of Chaucer's little impostures: the main source was Boccaccio; more exactly, Chaucer got his plot from the *Question d'Amore* of Menedon in the *Filocolo*,[2] not from the later version of the same story in the *Decameron*.[3] Several important elements were borrowed from other works, but only one of those secondary sources, viz., the *Historia* of Geoffrey of Monmouth, will have to be considered in the present study.

The story in the *Filocolo* is substantially the same as in the *Franklin's Tale*, except that the lady bids her lover stop wooing her until he can provide her in January with a garden blooming as in May. When he takes her to the garden she asks him not to claim his reward until her husband is away. She goes home, her husband notices her grief, and the story ends as in the *Franklin's Tale*.

Reserving for independent treatment the dramatic irony resulting in Chaucer's tale from his innovation as to the nature of the imposed task, we shall start with the less striking cases found in both the English and Italian versions.

The bare plot creates a series of contrasts between the expectations of the three men and the actual dénouement. The lover succeeds in accomplishing a task the reward of which he will not enjoy; the magician's efforts lead to the same result; and the husband's grief and resignation similarly contrast with the end. In the *Filocolo* little dramatic irony is derived from all this, first, because the different expectations and the feelings that accompany them are hardly more than the natural reactions to the situations; secondly, because the dénouement itself, far from striking us as the play of mysterious agents, is accepted as the outcome of conceivable or even

---

[1] Supported by W. H. Schofield in "Chaucer's *Franklin's Tale*," *P.M.L.A.*, XVI (1901), 405–49; by H. Cummings in *The Indebtedness of Chaucer's Works to the Italian Works of Boccaccio* (1916), chapter x, pp. 181–97; and by several others.

[2] *Opere volgari di Giovanni Boccaccio*, ed. by Moutier (Firenze, 1829), VIII, 48–60.

[3] *Decam.*, X, 5. See P. Rajna, "Le origini della novella narrata del 'Frankeleyn' nei *Canterbury Tales* del Chaucer," *Rom.*, XXXII (1903), 204–67; K. Young, "Chaucer's Use of Boccaccio's *Filocolo*," *Mod. Phil.*, IV (1906), 169–77, and *The Origin and Development of the Story of Troilus and Criseyde* (Ch. Soc., 1908), especially note to p. 181; A. Aman, *Die Filiation der "Frankeleynes Tale" in Chaucer's "Caunterbury Tales"* (Munich diss., 1912), pp. 128–29; J. S. P. Tatlock, *The Scene of the "Franklin's Tale" Visited* (Ch. Soc., 1914), pp. 55–75; and J. L. Lowes, "*The Franklin's Tale*, the *Teseide* and the *Filocolo*," *Mod. Phil.*, XV (1918), 689–728.

well-known psychological factors—loyalty to one's word, and the contagiousness of good. These remarks also apply to the *Franklin's Tale,* with this essential difference, that the characters have been given new life; our genuine interest, especially in Aurelius and the clerk of Orleans,[4] secures our attention for every ironic circumstance of their fate. While the Italian lover was little more than a type, the sufferings of Aurelius have become real to us, and we are kept aware of the irony, first of his despair, then of his exertions and sacrifices to deserve a reward which circumstances and the better part of his own nature will cause him to refuse when offered. Similarly, the Italian Tebano has developed into the shrewd magician of Orleans who so well knows how to lead up to the hour of bargaining, when he can afford to "make it straunge" and swear that he will not take less than a thousand pounds. Yet this true business man is going to release Aurelius from every penny of his debt.

But the best stroke of irony contained in the plot as common to Boccaccio and Chaucer is not in the parts of the men; it is in the heroine's answer to her lover. In her honest desire to rid herself of his attentions, she promises to yield if he accomplishes a task which she purposely chooses as impossible. He succeeds in performing it, so that her sincere attempt to discourage him gives him a right to claim her love. This is ironical enough in itself, but the paleness of Boccaccio's heroine greatly weakens—in fact, almost hides—this irony. The Italian lady weeps and maintains that she will commit suicide rather than go to her lover, but a moment later she obeys her husband so well indeed that she adorns herself for the occasion—"*ornatasi et fattasi bella.*"[5] For such a heroine, we are not likely to feel enough sympathy to stop and wonder at possible incongruities between her plans and their outcome. Nor does Boccaccio wish to have us stop and wonder;[6] the tale is primarily a *Question d'Amore* told with the purpose of opening a discussion on the three "gentle" deeds of the three men. All through the story, the woman is little more than an occasion for other people's generosity.

[4] Less dramatic irony is added by the characterization of Arveragus, partly because of his hope that "it may be wel, paraventure, yet to-day." Professor Hart calls it a "just foreknowledge of what Aurelius will do," which perhaps would not be entirely consistent with Chaucer's praise of the "freedom" of Arveragus as implicit in the question at the end. I would rather call it a faint hope. See W. M. Hart, *The "Franklin's Tale" Considered as a Masterpiece of Narrative Art* (Haverford Essays, 1909), pp. 183–234, especially pp. 190–91.

[5] Boccaccio has taken good care to change this in his later version (*Decam.,* X, 5): "venuta la seguente mattina, in su l'aurora, *senza troppo ornarsi, . . . . n'andò la donna* a casa messer Ansaldo."

[6] If he did, he would not take any chance, but would deliberately interrupt his story to comment on the incongruity. See chapter ii, pp. 14–16.

Chaucer's tale also is a *Question d'Amore,* but it is much more than that: the characters are developed for their own sake, the woman's figure, unimportant in the *Question* as such, being given the most attention and loving care. From the beginning we know Dorigen as the devoted and faithful wife who has lived so completely in her one great feeling that all the world beside has been perceived as in a dream, through a sort of morbid haze. Outside of Arveragus, people and things have interested her exactly to the extent of his relation to them. Because the rocks seem to threaten his life they are a terrible reality to her, but Aurelius might sigh for very long before being noticed. Only the plainest words have the power to wake her up. With an effort she shakes off her dream and, for the first time, really "looks upon Aurelius":

> "Is this your wil," quod she, "and sey ye thus?
> Never erst," quod she, "ne wiste I what ye mente."[7]

Our sympathy for Dorigen, our participation in all her sorrows and joys is insured from that moment. If she now softened her refusal by promising her love merely under the same condition as her Italian sister had (viz., if her suitor can provide her in January with a garden blooming as in May), we, the readers, half-suspecting that the task might be accomplished, would passionately wish to hold her back from uttering the fatal words. But Dorigen's answer differs from that of the Italian heroine in the nature of the task assigned, and this difference brings entirely new elements into the dramatic irony of the promise motif as found in the Italian —the question that we have reserved for independent treatment.[8]

To loving Dorigen, longing for the return of her husband from overseas, the "feendly grisly rokkes blake" have become an *idée fixe.* Why has God created this "werk unresonable"? She cannot answer the question,

> "But thilke god, that made wind to blowe,
> As kepe my lord! this my conclusioun."[9]

For one moment we have seen her "looking upon Aurelius," but her *idée fixe* was still there, struggling to reinvade the whole of her consciousness. Thus she not only chooses a seemingly impossible task, but the nature of it is dictated by her love for her husband; and it is that very task, completed long after the safe return of Arveragus, i.e., long after Dorigen will have ceased to care about the rocks at all, which will threaten to oblige her to

[7] F. 980–81.

[8] Much of what follows is suggested by Professor Tatlock's analysis of this beautiful stroke in "Astrology and Magic in Chaucer's *Franklin's Tale," Kittredge Anniversary Papers* (Boston, 1913), pp. 339 ff.

[9] F. 888–89.

yield to her unwelcome lover. There is not a line of comment on the part of the author, not one word of emphasis in which we hear his voice, not even one accent that can make us feel, between the tale and us, the poet's personal appreciation of the dramatic irony he has created. And perhaps this reticence should be taken as a hint: the depth, the beauty, and the pathos of such a stroke are hardly a matter for discussion. The subject, however, cannot be left without one word on the element which, to my mind, gives this particular case of dramatic irony its unique character in all the works of Chaucer: I mean the soothing influence spreading over the whole of the tale from an anticipation of its charming end. If Dorigen's love of her husband actually became the cause of an unwilling surrender to Aurelius, our response would be a feeling of revolt against the blind inhuman ruling powers.[10] But we know that "she may have bettre fortune" than we expected at first, and that knowledge creates a conciliating atmosphere in which even the mockery of Fortune loses its cruelty.

How did Chaucer come to make Dorigen assign to Aurelius the task of removing the rocks? The suggestion, Professor Tatlock tells us, may have come from Geoffrey of Monmouth, from those chapters of the *Historia Regum Britanniae* where Merlin transports from Ireland to England the huge rocks of the Dance of the Giants.[11] If we keep in mind that the king for whom Merlin performs the task is, like Dorigen's lover, called Aurelius; that another name, that of Arveragus, is found in both works; that the Latin form of the two names in the *Franklin's Tale* strongly suggests a Latin source;[12] that the existence of a Breton analogue in which Chaucer would have found the rock motif is discarded for good; and, finally, that Chaucer's previous acquaintance with the *Historia*[13] is not open to question—if we keep all these facts in mind, Dr. Tatlock's suggestion appears a very strong probability. In the same connection, I wish to draw attention to *Historia Regum Britanniae,* Book VIII, chapter 19, where Geoffrey tells us how King Uther falls in love with Igerna, whose husband then confines her to the castle of Tintagel. By magic, Merlin causes the king to assume the semblance of the husband, so that he can penetrate unhindered into the castle. The likeness with the *Franklin's Tale* is threefold: magic is used with the same end in view, viz., the fulfillment of a

---

[10] A feeling close to that experienced in reading Thomas Hardy.

[11] *Historia,* Book VIII, chapters 10–12. See J. S. P. Tatlock, *The Scene of the "Franklin's Tale" Visited,* p. 69, text and note 5. The episode had previously been mentioned in the same connection by Professor Schofield (*op. cit.,* pp. 417–18), but according to him Chaucer and Geoffrey of Monmouth show traces of the same old Celtic traditions, and there is no influence of the *Historia* on the *Fkl. T.*

[12] J. S. P. Tatlock, *op. cit.,* p. 68.

[13] See the *House of Fame,* l. 1470.

lover's desire; the scene, in both cases, is a lonely seashore castle;[14] and there is a resemblance between the names of the two women, "Igerna" and "Dorigen."[15] Now, in the somewhat dull account of wars that constitute the bulk of the *Historia,* the disguise of the king and the removal of the rocks are, apart from the prophecies, the only two magic achievements of Merlin.[16] Both occur in the same book, about ten pages apart. That one should remind us of the feat of the Orleans clerk both by the means employed and by the name of Aurelius, and the other by the end in view, the setting, and a certain resemblance in the names seems almost too much for mere accident, especially in the light of the other facts previously listed in favor of Professor Tatlock's suggestion.[17]

For our subject the interest of this tracing of the rock motif to its almost certain "source" lies in the fact that our conclusion leaves as mysterious and wonderful as ever the artist's insight into the dramatic possibilities of the suggestion. This was the insight of genius, of creative genius in the full sense of the term.

One word more on the bearing which our study of dramatic irony would have on the question of the main source—were that question not already solved! The critics who, for a long time, opposed the theory of Rajna on the Boccaccian origin of the tale used to lay stress on the removal of the rocks, a feature, they maintained, which Chaucer found in his lost Breton source. But the more we study Chaucer's treatment of dramatic irony in general, the less surprised we are to find him, with or without traceable suggestion, remodel a story for the sake of a fine ironical touch.

---

[14] *"Etenim situm est in mari, et undique circumclusum ab ipso, nec est introitus alter, nisi quem angusta rupes praebat: ipsum tres armati milites prohibere queunt: licet cum toto regno Britanniae astiteris"* (Book VIII, chapter 19). There may be some connection between that castle situated on a cliff and Chaucer's implication of a bold high shore at Penmark, a point in which his description is at variance with facts. See J. S. P. Tatlock, *op. cit.*, pp. 7–9.

[15] This, of course, in no way weakens the probability of the derivation of "Dorigen" from "Dorguen" or a similar form. See J. S. P. Tatlock, *op. cit.*, pp. 36–40.

[16] There is little magic beside that of Merlin. The Igerna episode also stands out because of the connection with the birth of Arthur.

[17] The Igerna episode is interesting also as a possible thread on which Chaucer's thoughts may have passed from Boccaccio's *Question d'Amore* to the Celtic world: one magical achievement for the fulfillment of a lover's desire—a rather unusual theme—was not unlikely to remind Chaucer of the same motif in the Igerna chapter. This magic feat of Merlin's may have brought back to the poet's memory (or made him re-read) the account of the other, i.e., the removal of the rocks. Exactly when the plan to give the story a Breton coloring may have originated, it would be difficult to guess, but a connection seems probable between that plan and the over-sea journey of Arveragus, for crossing the Channel in search of adventures was a very familiar feature of Breton stories (in Marie de France, *Milun* and *Eliduc*).

Even more: this masterly stroke may be in the spirit of the Breton bards and their French interpreters; it may fit perfectly in their beautiful dream world, full of deep and tragic irony.[18] Still, its beauty and pathos rest so entirely on appreciation of psychological values that, quite irrespective of other considerations, it seems less risky to credit Chaucer with the invention than to attribute it to one of his Breton or French masters.

---

[18] The extant Breton lays make frequent use of dramatic irony. I am not referring here to the part played by chance in *Guigemar, Le Freine,* or *Milun,* but to contrasts largely independent of the hazy supernatural background of the lays. I find three such strokes, not of the beauty and depth of Dorigen's request, yet of undeniable intensity, and, in one case (*Les dous amanz*), of real pathos (I am omitting *Equitan,* which is a miserable fabliau). (*a*) In *Milun,* the knight crosses the Channel to fight against a young man whose great fame has aroused his jealousy. At the same time he will look for his lost son, who, he knows, must be in France. Little does he suspect that his son and the brave knight are one and the same person (see *Die lais der Marie de France,* hrsg. von Karl Warnke [Halle, 1885 and 1925], pp. 164–65). (*b*) In *Le Freine,* a duchess accuses her friend who has given birth to twins on the ground that more than one child at a time is a sign of adultery. Afterward, she herself gives birth to twins (*op. cit.,* p. 57, especially ll. 81–88). (*c*) In *Les dous amanz,* an old king, out of selfish tenderness for his daughter, imposes upon her suitors the almost impossible task of carrying her to the top of a high hill without taking any rest. To him who can do it the princess will be married. The young knight she loves secures a magic drink which is to restore his forces as he ascends the hill. But, carried away by his hopes and enthusiasm, he does not feel his strength abating, and repeatedly declines to make use of the magic liquor. He reaches the top and dies exhausted (*op. cit.,* p. 121, especially ll. 221–29).

# VI. THE *NUN'S PRIEST'S TALE*

Comparatively little dramatic irony is found in the animal epic in general. Perhaps the genre offers too many opportunities for other forms of humor: veiled satire of human society, mock-heroic tone, conscious roguery, pictures of attitudes and gestures—all suggest themselves to the rimers more frequently and more naturally than the irony of action.[1] This general remark applies to the *Nun's Priest's Tale* in spite of the part played in it by two excellent cases of dramatic irony. The first is clearly taken from Chaucer's source, while the second seems to be largely his own contribution.

1. The reversal of parts of flatterer and dupe is the very core of the story. Good dramatic irony must inevitably result from any such reversal. In our fable, i.e., in the *Nun's Priest's Tale* and its analogues, this dramatic irony is heightened, first, by the character of the fox as accepted in animal epics. His reputation as archmaster in deception not only makes his failure more amusing in itself, but makes it appear as the almost direct consequence of his last piece of cunning. For where could the cock have learned to handle the subtle weapon of flattery better than in the first half of the story, where he falls a victim to the artfulness of the fox? And, secondly, the dramatic irony of the reversal is heightened—again in its analogues, as well as in the *Nun's Priest's Tale*—by the amusing similarity of methods used first by the fox against the cock, then vice versa: the eyes closed[2] in one episode, and the mouth open in the other.[3] All this is part of the story

---

[1] The strokes of the *Pèlerinage de Renart* (Branch VIII) are not as typical of the genre as, e.g., the misunderstandings created by the disguise of Renart (*Le roman de Renart,* pub. par Ernest Martin [Paris, 1882–87], I, 67–68).

[2] Within the first episode, Chaucer alone has the little extra irony of Chaunteceleer's readiness to follow the advice of Daun Russel, not only closing his eyes but stretching his neck, that neck by which the fox will catch him. The detail, of course, may be due entirely to Chaucer's own observation of a barnyard, but it may equally well have been suggested by some version lost to us. The catching by the throat, apparently remembered as a picturesque detail, is mentioned in several allusions to the episode (see *Le plai de Renart,* ed. Martin, Vol. I, p. 47, l. 1671, and a passage of the *Roman d'Alexandre,* quoted by B. ten Brink in *Or. and An.,* p. 114), though not in any of our versions of the story proper: the French *Renart* introduces the cock's neck only in descriptive passages (Martin, ll. 86, 242, 350 = *Or. and An.,* pp. 117 ff., ll. 1330, 1490, 1602), Marie de France does not mention it at all, and in *Reinhart Fuchs* the bird is caught *"bi dem houbete."*

[3] The similarity is better brought out in the *Renart* than in the *N.P.T.* Compare,

as handed down through centuries; in Chaucer's presentation of the ironical contrast I find no original feature.

2. The second effect of dramatic irony in the *Nun's Priest's Tale* comes from the feeling of security of both Chauntecleer and Pertelote just before the accident. The strong mind of Madame Pertelote is very much above superstition. Are not dreams easily accounted for on a rigorously scientific basis?

> "Alas! and conne ye been agast of swevenis?
> No-thing, god wot, but vanitee, in sweven is."[4]

Such feelings, and the solidity of Pertelote's information, are remembered with a smile when the dream comes true and our heroine shrieks "ful louder than dide Hasdrubales wyf." But the stronger and more humorous irony comes from the attitude of Chauntecleer himself, partly because a feeling of security is so much the opposite of his first natural reaction, partly because of the amusingly indirect way in which such a feeling is awakened in him. The wisdom of Pertelote has very little to do with it, for Chauntecleer, all through the argument about dreams, feels confident that he has the stronger support of authorities. That is exactly why he embarks on such a long and learned exposition of his views. The logical conclusion of his argument is, of course, that he should be on his guard. But it happens that, in the course of his speech, his pleasure in exhibiting his knowledge and cleverness has developed in him a certain self-satisfaction that quickly brings him to self-confidence. Because he has so brilliantly demonstrated that he should be afraid, he is not afraid any more! This change of mood calls for a change in the topic of conversation. Madame Pertelote is the natural subject, for the beautiful scarlet red around her eyes looks even more attractive now that Chauntecleer has recovered his sense of masculine superiority. The world around is full of joy, like Chauntecleer's own heart:

---

in Chaucer, B.4619–25 to *Renart,* ll. 446–52 (in *Or. and An.,* ll. 1698–1704) with its calculated repetition of the same words:

> "La boce," fait-il, "soit honie,
> *Qui s'entremet de* noise fere
> *A l'ore qu'*ele se doit tere."
> "Si soit" fet li cos, "con je voil.
> La male gote li cret l'oil
> *Qui s'entremet de* someller
> *A l'ore que* il doit veillier."

The corresponding passage in *Reinhart Fuchs* (ll. 161–69) does not bring out the parallelism at all.

[4] B.4111–12.

"I am so ful of Ioye and of solas
That I defye bothe sweven and dreem . . . ."[5]

And on his toos he rometh up and doun,
Him deyned not to sette his foot to grounde . . . .[6]

and Chauntecleer so free
Song merier than the mermayde in the see; . . . .[7]

But the reader knows what to expect in the next lines:

No-thing ne liste him thanne for to crowe,
But cryde anon, "cok, cok," and up he sterte,
As man that was affrayed in his herte.[8]

The whole episode, from Chauntecleer's dream to the realization of it, strikes the reader as typically Chaucerian and very likely to be our poet's own contribution. One feels that such sustained humor, based chiefly on characterization, would be exceptional in the literary genre to which the source of the *Nun's Priest's Tale* belonged. But what was that source exactly? If, as I am strongly inclined to believe, M. Foulet is right in considering the second branch of the French *Renart* as an original work of art,[9] no antecedent of it can be claimed as the source of the *Nun's Priest's Tale*, and the version used by Chaucer is our own familiar *Renart*.[10] In that case, the dramatic irony of Chauntecleer's feeling of security is entirely Chaucer's creation. He received at the most a few vague hints. Dame Pinte, in the French, is a pale and inconsistent figure. At the beginning of the tale she is of average timidity.[11] Later, she comforts Chantecler:

"Mau fetes qui vos esmaies. ...
Vos resembles le chen qui crie
Ains que la pierre soit coüe."[12]

This reminds us somewhat of Pertelote, but the similarity stops here, for

[5] B. 4360–61. [6] B. 4370–71. [7] B. 4459–60. [8] B. 4466–68.

[9] Lucien Foulet, *Le roman de Renart* (Paris, 1914). See also I. C. Lecompte, "Chaucer's *Nonne Prestes Tale* and the *Roman de Renard*," *Mod. Phil.*, XIV (1917), 737–49. M. Foulet is not concerned with the bearing of his theory on the question of source of the *N.P.T.*, but Mr. Lecompte re-examines the problem treated by Miss K. Petersen (*On the Sources of the "Nonne Prestes Tale"* [Boston, 1898]) and, taking up her arguments one by one, arrives at the conclusion that there is no sufficient reason, in a comparison of the *N.P.T.*, *Reinhart Fuchs*, and the *Renart*, for assuming French versions of the cock and fox story earlier than our second branch.

[10] The fable of Marie de France can be left out of consideration in this study. Chaucer may have known it, but the thirty-eight lines cannot have offered him any dramatic irony missing in his longer source.

[11] Ll. 93–97. [12] Ll. 179–83.

Pinte strongly believes in the significance of dreams.[13] Scepticism is the part of Chantecler,[14] but his character is not conceived any more strongly than that of Pinte. He wavers between pale fears and pale comfort; nothing suggests that he feels particularly happy before the catastrophe.

But we cannot be absolutely sure that Chaucer followed the second branch of the *Renart* as we have it. According to Miss Petersen, the preserved French text and the *Nun's Priest's Tale* would both be derived from an earlier version. How much characterization would Chaucer have found in that source? Miss Petersen has noted seven points in which the *Nun's Priest's Tale* and *Reinhart Fuchs* agree with each other and differ from the French *Renart*. The sixth of these points is the following:

> The poet of *Reinhart* shows the same tendency to treat his cock and hen as human personages that Chaucer shows throughout. Pinte begs Schantecler to take care of himself for his children's sake, and pictures her distress as a bereft wife if his recklessness leads him to destruction. The cock's sense of humor . . . . is in the same strain. This peculiarity of style, . . . . is a trait which Chaucer's original may have shared with the original of *Reinhart Fuchs*.[15]

It is thus not entirely impossible that Chaucer's source may have given him, for the characterization on which our dramatic contrast is resting, a somewhat more distinct suggestion than could be found in the extant version of the *Renart*.

One word more on a feature that does *not* affect the dramatic irony of the *Nun's Priest's Tale*. The address to Destiny that cannot be avoided,[16] the reference to Fortune,[17] and the seventeen lines on predestination[18] remind us of *Troilus and Criseyde* and of the fatalistic background which in that poem lends such dignity and impressiveness to the ironies of life. But the passages in the *Nun's Priest's Tale* are mock-heroic and of course build no background at all. Their delightful humor has nothing in common with the dramatic irony of the tale.

To sum up, just as in the treatment of the fabliaux, Chaucer has taken from the source of the *Nun's Priest's Tale* the dramatic irony resulting from the contrast of situation with situation. What he has created, or at least developed a great deal, is a subtler contrast of situation with characters and moods.

---

[13] On Chaucer's interest in the character of the sceptical woman as a reason for his innovation here, see K. Petersen, *op. cit.*, pp. 92 and 94–95.

[14] Ll. 259 ff.

[15] Kate O. Petersen, *op. cit.*, pp. 85–86.

[16] B. 4528. [17] B. 4593–94. [18] B. 4424–40.

# VII. THE *PARDONER'S TALE*

## Dramatic Irony in Chaucer's Source

Only the closest analogues to the *Pardoner's Tale* will be taken into consideration: (*a*) The end of an Italian miracle of the fifteenth century entitled *Rappresentazione di Sant' Antonio*;[1] (*b*) a play of Hans Sachs, *Der Dot im Stock*;[2] (*c*) an Italian *novella* of the thirteenth or fourteenth century, *Qui conta d'uno romito*;[3] and (*d*) an *exemplum* found in a 1406 manuscript and printed by Mr. J. Klapper as Number 98 of his collection of *exempla* from manuscripts in the University of Breslau library.[4] We shall refer to this *exemplum* as B . 98. The following summary applies to these four versions and to Chaucer's:

Three companions (robbers, revelers or merchants) meet a man (a hermit or simply an old man) who tells them where Death abides, either directing them to the spot or warning them against it. The three companions go to the place and find gold. One of the three goes to buy food and poisons it in order to get rid of the other two. While he is on his errand, his two companions decide to kill him as soon as he returns. They do so; then they eat the poisoned food and die.

Let us first see how much dramatic irony is contained in the longer analogues, the Italian and German plays.

At every step in his play the author of the Italian miracle delights in showing us his three sinners played upon by a kind of weird, cruelly humorous Fate. We notice at the very opening the happy anticipations of Caraparello;[5] the insistence laid by Tagliagambe on the buying of enough wine and the bringing of scales to weigh the gold;[6] the weakness of

[1] Alessandro d'Ancona, *Sacre rappresentazioni dei secoli XIV, XV e XVI* (Firenze, 1872), II, 33–63.

[2] Neudrücke deutscher Litteraturwercke (Halle, 1886), Nos. 60–61, pp. 94–106.

[3] *Qui conta d'uno romito che andando per un luogo foresto trovo molto grande tesoro, Libro di novelle e di bel parlar gentile* (Firenze, 1572), novella 82, p. 86; reprinted in *Or. and An.*, pp. 132–33. On the date of this *novella*, found in the 1572 edition only (the 1525 *Cento novelle antiche* contained the version printed in *Or. and An.*, p. 131), see H. S. Canby, "Some Comments on the Sources of Chaucer's *Pardoner's Tale*," *Mod. Phil.*, II (1905), 477–87, especially p. 479, and A. d'Ancona, *Del Novellino e delle sue fonti*, Studj di critica e storia letteraria, parte seconda (Bologna, 1912), p. 5. In this same work, see pages 136–38 for references to numerous analogues to the *Pd. T.*

[4] *Exempla aus Handschriften des Mittelalters*, hrsg. von Joseph Klapper, Sammlung Mittelalterlicher Texte (Heidelberg, 1911). On this collection, see T. F. Crane, "New Analogues of Old Tales," *Mod. Phil.*, X (1913), 301–16, especially p. 310.

[5] P. 53.

[6] P. 55.

Scaramuccia's distrust of the other two (much more ironical than simple confidence);[7] the two murderers' enjoyment of their hearty meal, with especial commendation of their victim's taste in wines; their indulgence in bright plans just when the poison begins to work; and, finally, the state of helplessness in which they find themselves in spite of their wealth.[8] As these different ironical touches follow one another in quick succession, stirring up our sense both of the incongruous and of poetic justice, we may or may not notice the more essential tragedy of the robbers' quest of Death, that quest which must result in their finding Death indeed, though in a very unexpected way. The author betrays hardly any perception of this irony. He neither prepares for it by emphasis on the quest episode,[9] nor does he do anything to insure our recollection of the first element of the contrast —the quest—when the dénouement brings in the second—death.[10]

As implied by the title of Sachs's play, *Der Dot im Stock,* the irony of the quest motif is given much more emphasis than in the Italian miracle. Not that there is any long or deliberate quest: immediately after having killed the hermit, the three start on their way:

> Kumbt! wollen zu dem stock uns nehen
> Und den dot auch darin pesehen[11]

and a few lines below:

> Pocz marter, schawt! hie ligt kain dot,
> Sunder pey dawsent guelden rot[12]

but the warning of the hermit is recalled many times in the course of the play:

> Der dot wirt uns dreyen gar sues,
> Dar wir darfon drincken und essen.[13]

Barrabas, sending Jesmas for food, advises him to be careful and avoid the "stadtknecht":

> Sunst kom wir all mit dir in not
> Und wer in stock gewest der dot.[14]

---

[7] P. 56.

[8] P. 61.

[9] There is no deliberate purpose in the quest; it is started by mere chance.

[10] The contrast is dismissed in the following lines, pp. 54–55:

> "Guardate, frate' mio, quanta pazia
> Regna in quel pazerel, vecchio eremita,
> Dicendo che era qua la morte ria!
> E' chiama morte quello che è vita.
> Se noi non venavam per questa via,
> Nostra ventura era per noi fallita."

[11] Ll. 165–66.

[12] Ll. 171–72.

[13] Ll. 176–77.

[14] Ll. 191–92.

Just after drinking the poisoned wine Dismas says:

> Wen wir habn gessn und druncken gnunck,
> Den wollen wir dailen des schacz
> Im stock, dem dot zu drucz und dracz.[15]

And finally the truth of the hermit's words is acknowledged and stressed by the dying Barrabas:

> Der alt schalk in dem graben rock
> Hat noch war gsagt, das in dem stock
> Der grewlich dot verporgen sey, . . . .[16]

To this central piece of gruesome, tragic irony, Hans Sachs adds several touches of secondary importance: it is when fleeing from Death that the hermit meets it at the hands of the robbers;[17] while Dismas is stating his main reason for wishing to kill Jesmas, viz., the fear that he may weaken and betray his companions, this overscrupulous Jesmas is buying the poison. The irony of the thieves' expectations is allowed much stress in lines 214–19, 240, 254–62, and—still more strikingly—in lines 274–87, spoken while the poisoned wine is being drunk.

Comparing the Italian miracle with Sachs's play, we find that they have in common only the two ironical circumstances inseparable from the barest outline of the story, viz., that of the quest of Death, and that of the disappointment of the robbers' hopes. For all the other contrasts involving dramatic irony, we cannot tell whether the common ancestor of those two versions offered any more than a favorable frame.

How many of these secondary touches of dramatic irony were found in Chaucer's source? Our answer depends on the literary genre to which we assign that lost version. There are two possibilities: (*a*) an *exemplum;* and (*b*) a tale of some length, fabliau or *novella,* known either directly or through English translation. In favor of the *exemplum,* we have the antecedent probability, viz., the fact that Chaucer was rather likely to make his Pardoner tell a story from a book of *exempla,*[18] the practical certainty that he did consult Thomas of Cantimpré in connection with the tale,[19] the verbal parallelism between Chaucer's and Sachs's wording of a moral most suitable to an *exemplum,*[20] and, finally, the closeness of the

[15] Ll. 278–80. [16] Ll. 201–3.

[17] Ll. 152, 167.

[18] The more so as the Pardoner is really delivering a sermon. See C. O. Chapman, "*The Pardoner's Tale:* A Mediaeval Sermon," *Mod. Lang. Notes,* XLI (1926), 506–9.

[19] See K. Petersen, *op. cit.,* note 3 to p. 97.

[20] "Radix malorum est cupiditas" (C. 334, 426) and "Wan geicz ist ein wurczl aller suent" (l. 319). B. 98 is entitled "Exemplum de Auaricia."

*Pardoner's Tale* to one of the known *exempla,* our B . 98.[21] These facts, of course, do not exclude the possibility of Chaucer's acquaintance with another form of the story,[22] but they certainly establish a very strong probability in favor of an *exemplum* text as responsible for the poet's choice of the theme. Now a rimer of fabliaux would almost certainly have delighted in accumulating contrasts of the nature of those found in the Italian miracle, and any author of *novelle* would, at the very least, have emphasized the hopes and disappointment of his heroes as does our version of the *Libro di novelle.*[23] On the contrary, an *exemplum,* because of the brevity and compactness characteristic of the genre, must be imagined as giving no space at all to such secondary touches of dramatic irony as those noted in the two plays, and probably very little attention (if any) to the contrasts of the men's hopes and efforts with their fate.[24] Thus, it seems reasonable to imagine, if not the one source, at least one of the sources used by Chaucer as containing only one really striking touch of dramatic irony, viz., the contrast of the companions' quest of Death with their finding death indeed, though in quite another sense. Standing alone, the irony involved in this contrast would, of course, draw the reader's attention the more surely. This is exactly what happens in our *exemplum* B . 98. As this text appears to me to have the best claims to a close analogy with

---

21 Our summary given above (see p. 72) would not apply to the other known *exempla,* viz., No. 97 of J. Klapper's collection, and three unpublished versions found in manuscripts *Add. 27336, Add. 11872,* and *Harl. 3938* of the British Museum and mentioned by J. A. Herbert on pages 660, 693, and 711 of Volume III of his *Catalogue of Romances in the Department of Manuscripts in the British Museum* (London, 1910). In none of these four versions are the companions told about the abode of Death. In B . 97 there is nobody to warn the avaricious men or comment on their finding the gold. In *Add. 11872* a philosopher warns his disciples against different sins, not against death. This is also the case in *Add. 27336,* where the part of the philosopher is played by Christ. Finally, in *Harl. 3938,* Christ calls the sack of money death itself, but, since his disciples are with him when the treasure is first noticed, there is no occasion for the quest-of-death motif. In these four *exempla* the covetous companions are two (instead of three in B . 98 and the *Pd. T.*).

22 This is no more than a possibility. The arguments formerly used to support it were: (*a*) the fact that no collection of *exempla* presented any related theme, but we have seen that this is no longer true; and (*b*) the location in Flanders (on this point, see K. Petersen, *op. cit.,* note 3 to p. 97).

23 *"& molto si cominciarono a rallegrare, & a fare insieme grande sollazzo."* On both sides, the companions congratulate themselves on the course they have decided to take: *"Io saro poi il piu ricco huomo di tutto questo paese,"* and *"sara poi tra noi due tutto questo grande hauere ..."* And, in conclusion, *"l'oro rimase libero come di primer."*

24 Though this irony always remains, since it is inherent in the plot.

Chaucer's source,[25] I shall give it here in full as printed in Mr. Klapper's *Exempla*, only italicizing the passages that interest us especially in connection with dramatic irony:

De tribus sociis, qui thesaurum invenerunt. Exemplum de Auaricia. *Quidam heremita* volens in nemore ortum edificare ex casu fodiendo *invenit thezaurum statimque clamauit ter magna voce: Mors, mors, mors! Pretereuntes vero tres socij mercatores venerunt dicentes: Ubi est mors, quam clamasti? Ille vero monstrauit eis thezaurum* et statim eum abinde repulerunt. Qui recedens venit ad cellam suam. Isti vero cogitantes, quid essent facturi, ordinauerunt, ut vnus ex illis in ciuitatem iret et expensas aportaret. Eo uero abeunte cogittauerunt, ut eum, cum foueam descenderet, interficerent. Ipse uero vadens eciam cogitauit de perdicione istorum duorum, venenumque comparans omnia cibaria intoxicauit veniensque ad illos dixit: Volumusne prius comedere uel thezaurum excipere? Qui responderunt: Prius thezaurum excipiemus. Feceruntque illum ad foueam descendere, ut eum occiderent. Descendente vero eo *ipsum occiderunt et ipsi* postmodum comedentes *ambo mortui sunt et sic thezaurum intactum reliquerunt. Quo cum heremita (dum) venisset et eos mortuos vidisset, ait: Vere non est alius thezaurus nisi periculum et mors.*

To close this section, if Chaucer's one source had been a version as rich in secondary ironical implications as, let us say, the Italian miracle,

---

[25] The Italian *Qui conta d'uno romito* is found in an older manuscript, but it is a *novella,* not an *exemplum,* and this makes its claim much weaker than those of B . 98. Also, though four times as long as B . 98, it does not possess, in common with the *Pd. T.,* any striking feature not found in B . 98 as well.

But, if B . 98 has, of all extant texts, the best claims to close analogy with Chaucer's source, these claims still remain somewhat limited. For, in several details, the *Pd. T.* strikingly agrees with the Italian miracle, while in others it agrees with the play of Hans Sachs. In common with the miracle, it has: the drawing of lots, the mention of rats in the poison-buying scene, the promise of secrecy at the opening of the two murderers' conversation, and, in the same conversation, their plan of attacking only after the victim is seated (see H. S. Canby, *op. cit.*). In common with Hans Sachs it has: the moral at the end, the nature—gulden or florins—of the treasure, and its location in or under a tree (see W. M. Hart, "The 'Pardoner's Tale' and 'Der Dot im Stock'," *Mod. Phil.,* IX [1911], 17–22; other similarities are listed by Professor Hart, but I am inclined to think of them as accidental resemblances resulting from parallel attempts to vitalize the story). These secondary features found in the *Pd. T.* and in one of its longer analogues seem too numerous and of too definite a character to be explained away by mere chance. Since B . 98 does not contain any of them, two possibilities are left (taking for granted that Chaucer did use an *exemplum*): (*a*) Chaucer's *exemplum* was supplemented with some other version that supplied most of the concrete details listed above. In this case, the *exemplum* may have been, even in its details, very close to B . 98. (*b*) Chaucer's *exemplum* was the one source of his *Pd. T.;* but then that one source must have contained several details different from those in B . 98. This hypothetical *exemplum* would not have to be imagined as longer or more circumstantial than the typical *exemplum,* which is short, but compact and full of concrete details. Notice, for instance, the number of particulars crowded in B . 97. (One of them, the feigned playing that leads to the murder, is familiar to us as part of the *Pd. T.*)

our quest-of-Death tale (admitting that the theme would have been selected at all) might have been quite different from what it is. But if we are right in believing that Chaucer knew a version where dramatic irony was treated very much as in the *exemplum* just quoted, little or no work of elimination was required of our poet before he could concentrate his full attention on the development of the one tragic irony of the plot.

## Dramatic Irony in Chaucer's Version

In Chaucer's tale, the secondary ironic possibilities of the theme are completely sacrificed in favor of the one really tragic motif of the quest of Death. That the author of the *Merchant's* and the *Franklin's Tales* was capable of detecting and developing those secondary possibilities is obvious enough. We have to admit that he deliberately sacrificed all the contrasts that depended mostly on human actions and their consequences because he preferred to emphasize fully the one contrast in which Fate itself was seen at work. How did he make this the central feature of his story?

First of all, he realized that there was little contrast between a short and quite accidental quest of Death by companions who, one minute before, were ready for any adventure whatever—as is the case in all known analogues—and the fact that on that quest they actually meet their death. How much more tragic and intense if the three companions could be given a real reason why they should start on a mad and feverish, though consistent and deliberate, quest of Death! What associations of ideas brought the specific details of the tavern scene in Flanders during a pestilence it is impossible to ascertain. And it matters little here; the important point is the admirable skill with which Chaucer uses these new details to create the proper atmosphere, an atmosphere of heavy fear and sin, the mood of a *Danse macabre,* with the horror of Death increased by his mysterious character.

This background created, Chaucer tells us how his three "riotours" swear to find "this false traytour death" and to kill him who has slain so many of their friends, and how they proceed on their way, sticking to their purpose in their obstinacy of rioters "al dronken":

> And many a grisly ooth than han they sworn,
> And Cristes blessed body they to-rente—
> "Deeth shal be deed, if that they may him hente."[26]

The enigmatic character of the old man they meet on their way, the lines in which one of the revelers—perhaps not wrongly—accuses him of being the spy of Death, and the veiled challenge (or warning?) of the old man—

[26] C. 708–10.

"Nat for your boost he wol him no-thing hyde"[27] (a retort, perhaps, to the rioters' question, "Why artow al forwrapped save thy face?")[28]—all this contributes to heighten the impression and keep up the great "leitmotiv" Death.

The three revelers proceed till they come to that tree under which the reader, just like the revelers themselves, half expects to find the grim reaper with his scythe. He is accordingly quite prepared to identify with Death whatever will be found under that tree. Here again we must commend the skilful way in which Chaucer has kept us in suspense: in all the other versions we know beforehand that the three companions are to find a heap of gold, and, if we are to notice the connection between the short quest of Death, that heap of gold, and the end of the story, we must be reminded now and then that there is such a connection. This is Hans Sachs's technique; it verges on artificiality; the author's personality is distinctly perceived between the object and us. But Chaucer has done enough by way of preparation and he knows that we cannot miss the irony. One line more is enough, a line that needs no commentary:

> No lenger thanne after Deeth they soughte.[29]

They do not seek him any more; they do not even remember him. This complete forgetfulness is infinitely more tragic than the mood of defiant security of Sachs's robbers. They, at least, kept repeating that they had not found Death after all, showing thereby that they were still somewhat on their guard, that Fate could not have taken them entirely by surprise.

Chaucer's revelers forget Death, but the reader does not. He is hurried through the last episodes without any secondary touch of dramatic irony to distract his attention from the fulfillment of the grim prophecy.[30] From that moment on, everything Chaucer says is a definite step toward that fulfillment, and is felt as such. Fate, we know, is at work.

---

[27] C. 764. There is another such veiled threat in C. 747:

> "I yeve yow reed,
> Ne dooth un-to an old man noon harm now,
> Na-more than ye wolde men dide to yow
> In age, *if that ye so longe abyde.*"

[28] C. 718.

[29] C. 772.

[30] In exactly ten lines (C. 879–88) the one who has been sent for food is killed, the other two sit down to their meal, drink the poisoned wine, and die. The irony of their expectations is dismissed in two lines:

> "Now lat us sitte and drinke, and make us merie
> And afterward we wol his body berie."
> —C. 883–84

It could hardly be less.

Fate or the Christian God? Though the *Pardoner's Tale* is a sermon, there is room for doubt. We shall see later[31] that the background of accepted Christian faith is about the least favorable background possible for dramatic irony. The only form it allows is poetic justice, and that only as far as the punishment of the wicked goes. The irony of the *Pardoner's Tale* is obviously more than that. Punishing the revelers for their sins could be called poetic justice, but starting them on a deliberate quest for Death is creating a luxury of contrast to be enjoyed for its own sake, independently of moral values.[32] Chaucer, the great dramatic artist, has emphasized the tragically ironic side of this story so much that he has overstepped a little, I fear, the bounds of classical sermon literature. The mysterious old man helps to carry us into a country of doubtful religious coloring.[33] We do not feel quite sure that the power behind the curtain is clearly and plainly the Christian God as chastiser of the wicked. Like Death in the tale, that power is impressive in proportion to its enigmatical character.

---

[31] Chapter ix, pp. 91–92.

[32] To a far less extent, this remark applies to Chaucer's source and to B . 98, for the moral lesson—avarice punished by death—comes out just as clearly where there is no quest of death at all, as in B . 97 and in the version of the *Cento novelle antiche* (*Or. and An.*, p. 131).

[33] The story is almost certainly of Eastern origin. See H. S. Canby, *op. cit.*

## VIII. THE FRAME OF THE *CANTERBURY TALES*

In the pilgrims' short and accidental relations to one another—relations that involve no action but only talk—there obviously was not much chance for dramatic irony.[1] Chaucer found one opportunity in a few little misreadings of character by that professional master of ceremonies, the host himself: his instinctive distrust of the narrative ability of Geoffrey Chaucer[2] (part of our poet's device to avoid putting himself in serious competition with his fellow-pilgrims), his fear that the Clerk who rides "so coy and still" might try to make the pilgrims weep for their sins,[3] and, finally, his evident anticipation of a *Monk's Tale* very different in character from that solemn sequence of "tragedies" in which he will find "no desport ne game."[4]

As part of the frame, we must treat here the ironical situations of the pilgrims' previous lives as presented in short narratives inserted in the different prologues and links.

First of all, the host's amusingly boastful attitude, "For I am perilous with knyf in honde,"[5] creates a delightful contrast with what he himself has just told us: his wife, he feels sure, will make him kill one of his neighbors some day.

Clearer still is the irony of the thanks with which the master of the Reeve accepts loans of the money pilfered from him.[6] The interesting point to remember in this connection is Chaucer's ability to create a situation worthy of the very best fabliaux. He had, of course, no chance of developing its possibilities in the Prologue.

But the deepest and most complex of these ironic strains of the pilgrims' lives comes from the Wife's relation to her three old husbands in contrast with her later very different attitude toward their young suc-

[1] If we accept Professor Tupper's view, that Chaucer "with delightfully suggestive irony . . . . opposed practice to precept, rule of life to dogma, by making several of his story tellers incarnate the very sins that they explicitly condemn," then the *Physician's Tale,* the *Second Nun's Tale,* etc., are from beginning to end dramatic irony of the same kind as the friar's sermon against anger in the *Sum. T.* But many strong objections can be raised against Professor Tupper's theory. See F. Tupper, "Chaucer and the Seven Deadly Sins," *P.M.L.A.,* XXIX (1914), 93–128; and "Chaucer's Sinners and Sins," *J.E.G.P.,* XV (1916), 56–106; and the refutation of the theory by J. L. Lowes, "Chaucer and the Seven Deadly Sins," *P.M.L.A.,* XXX (1915), 237–371, and by Koch, *Angl. Beibl.,* XXV (1914), 327–32, and XXVIII (1917), 152–55.

[2] B. 1895–1901. [3] E. 1–20. [4] B. 3114–54 and 3970–95.

[5] B. 3109. [6] General Prologue, ll. 609–12.

cessors. Many details may have been borrowed from Jean de Meung, but the highly dramatic situation is all Chaucer's. The first three husbands were good, i.e., rich, old, and very much in love:

> Me neded nat do lenger diligence
> To winne hir love, or doon hem reverence.[7]

With the fourth, however, the parts are reversed:

> I trowe I loved him beste, for that he
> Was of his love daungerous to me.[8]

Perfectly at ease as to the fidelity of her old husbands, the Wife has thought it good policy to rave against their supposed faithlessness.[9] It is as though Fate were answering a kind of challenge: her fourth husband is exactly what she had accused his predecessors of being:

> I hadde in herte greet despyt
> That he of any other had delyt.[10]

The Wife's reasons for marrying her first three husbands were far from disinterested; the victims were "gode, and riche, and olde,"[11] with the anticipated result that their tormentor is left a widow "faire, and riche, and yong, and wel bigoon."[12] But she soon falls in love with Jankin the clerk,

> And to him yaf I al the lond and fee
> That ever was me yeven ther-bifore.[13]

Here again the Wife is punished as if by a methodic reversal of rôles. On these repeated contrasts, not a word of comment. Indeed the best part of the joke lies in the fact that the Wife is only dimly conscious of it herself. It is a joke certainly, and humor is the dominant tone. And yet there is so much human truth in the account of the Wife's sentimental experiences; there is, flashing up here and there, so much of the heart-rending pathos of the flight of years, that we cannot help seeing a tragic side to the taming of the mature woman, who yesterday was still reveling in the powers of her beauty and youth. This is not the dramatic irony of the fabliaux; it is felt by too warm, too sympathizing a heart.

For the present study, the special interest of the frame as compared to the tales lies in Chaucer's more unquestionably independent creation of situations involving dramatic irony of the finest character. Our poet had good reasons for making use of his inventiveness here; he knew how much

---

[7] D. 205–6. [8] D. 513–14. [9] D. 393 ff. [10] D. 481–82.
[11] D. 197. [12] D. 606. [13] D. 630–31.

humor and life the use of the device could bring into the pilgrims' group. But are we sure that artistic considerations can give us the whole explanation of the relatively frequent occurrence of dramatic irony in the frame? This frame, we must remember, is Chaucer's most realistic piece of work. Perhaps a mental habit of including life's little ironies in his conception of real life may have led our poet to multiply his strokes in this particular portion of the *Canterbury Tales.*

## IX. NARRATIVES WITH LITTLE OR NO DRAMATIC IRONY

The narratives in which Chaucer disregards opportunities for dramatic irony afford additional proof of our poet's deliberate calculation of effects wherever he does make use of the device. For in only two cases, the *Legend of Good Women* and the *Manciple's Tale* (in neither of which Chaucer's narrative powers are at their best), does the absence of dramatic irony suggest lack of interest. In the other tales we feel that the use of the device would have added nothing of any value, or, indeed, in specific cases, would have spoiled the effect intended.

### THE "LEGEND OF GOOD WOMEN" AND THE "MANCIPLE'S TALE"

Chaucer's "Good Women" are not only women faithful in love but martyrs to the cause of love. Hence, two acts in the tragedy of each legend: confidence and cheerful anticipations in the first; separation by desertion and death in the second. No theme could have offered clearer or easier opportunities for dramatic irony. More than that, most of the sources used by Chaucer, especially Ovid and Virgil, supplied him with these ironical contrasts ready-made, emphatically stressing them by rhetorical clash of words. In spite of this—or perhaps on account of this—they almost entirely failed to arouse Chaucer's sense of the dramatic. One example will suffice, that of *Philomela*.[1]

When Tereus, having conceived his criminal plans, prays King Pandion to let Philomela visit her sister Progne, Chaucer summarizes the situation in two lines:

> And with his wyles kneled so and preyde,
> Til at the laste Pandion thus seyde: . . . .[2]

The corresponding scene of the *Metamorphoses* brings out the irony of Tereus' success. Made eloquent by the very intensity of his criminal passion, he is praised as a kind husband:

> et agit sua vota sub illa.
> Facundum faciebat amor: quotiensque rogabat
> Ulterius iusto, Prognen ita velle ferebat;
> Addidit et lacrimas, tamquam mandasset et illas.
> Pro superi, quantum mortalia pectora caecae
> Noctis habent! ipso sceleris molimine Tereus
> Creditur esse pius laudemque a crimine sumit.[3]

---

[1] Legend VII, ll. 2228–2393.

[2] Ll. 2294–95.

[3] *Metamorphoses*, Bk. VI, ll. 468–74.

To the prayers of Tereus, the Philomela of both versions adds her own. In the *Legend of Good Women,* however, the irony could be felt only on a second reading, for the request of the young woman occurs before Tereus conceives his plan. Nor does Chaucer show any appreciation of the irony.[4] But in the *Metamorphoses*:

> . . . . ut eat visura sororem,
> Perque suam contraque suam petit ipsa salutem . . . .
> Vincitur ambarum genitor prece; gaudet agitque
> Illa patri grates et successisse duabus
> Id putat infelix quod erit lugubre duabus.[5]

The next day King Pandion intrusts Philomela to the care of Tereus. In Chaucer, there is no more irony than is inherent in the plot. The king takes his children to the harbor,

> And turneth hoom; no malice he ne thoghte.[6]

In Ovid, Pandion first says that he will let Philomela go, since both his daughters and also Tereus desire it; he insists on her being sent back as soon as possible, and crowns his speech by demanding the right hands of Tereus and Philomela and joining them together:

> "Hanc ego, care gener, quoniam pia causa coegit,
> Ut voluere ambae, voluisti tu quoque, Tereu,
> Do tibi . . . ."
> Utque fide pignus dextras utriusque proposcit,
> Inter seque datas junxit . . . .[7]

And, finally, Chaucer skips Ovid's remarks on Progne's tears when she hears the false news of her sister's death:

> Et luget non sic lugendae fata sororis.[8]

The rest of Ovid's story—Progne's revenge—finds no place in this praise of virtuous women, but it may be worth noting that a web of irony covers the second act of the Latin narrative as well as the first.[9] One cannot help feeling puzzled at Chaucer's rejection, here as in most of the other legends,[10] not only of all comments on Fate, but of all the tragic irony so

[4] Ll. 2284–87. [5] Ll. 476–85. [6] L. 2307.

[7] Ll. 496–507. [8] L. 570. [9] Ll. 580, 624 ff., 650 ff.

[10] See, e.g., Chaucer's colorless rendering (ll. 1146–49) of the lines where Virgil (*Aeneid,* I, 709–21) insists on the irony of Dido's tenderness for the false Iulus, the god of love who is just wounding her; or, in *Lucretia,* the omission of Ovid's comments (*Fasti,* II, 789–90) on the reception of Tarquinius at the house of Calatyn, and on the success which will cost him his crown; or again, in *Hypsiphyle and Medea,* Guido's remarks (*Historia Trojana,* I–III), not paralleled in the English, about the foolishness of the old king who exposes his daughter to the dangers of love. In other cases, the sources had not stressed the irony of situations, and Chaucer followed them without any addition in that respect.

strongly emphasized by his source. Condensation could hardly account for these omissions,[11] and one isolated case, that of *Ariadne,* proves that Chaucer did not regard dramatic irony as incompatible with proper treatment of his subject, i.e., with due emphasis on the virtues of his heroines. This legend is especially interesting for us because its plot so strikingly recalls that of *Philomela.* But here—in the case of *Ariadne*—none of the possible sources shows any appreciation of dramatic contrasts, and it is our poet who brings out the irony of action, first, when his heroine arouses her sister Phaedra's interest in poor imprisoned Theseus, whose passion for that same Phaedra will later cause the catastrophe;[12] secondly, when Ariadne, as she offers to marry the noble prisoner, keeps pushing Phaedra to the foreground in all her plans;[13] and, finally, when the heroine expresses satisfaction with regard to the future that she has prepared for both her sister and herself.[14] As Professor Lowes has shown,[15] the setting of the scenes in which Chaucer introduces the motifs just mentioned was almost certainly suggested by Boccaccio's *Teseide.* Just the setting; and yet, one cannot help wondering how much, by association of ideas or rather of moods, reawakened and refreshed memories of Boccaccio's magic world may have influenced Chaucer in this case.[16] Whether it dealt with antiquity or not, that world was so much more real to Chaucer than Ovid's or Virgil's. For looking at the *Legend of Good Women* as a whole, one feels that Chaucer's blindness, or at least his indifference, to the ironical features so forcefully brought out in his sources would be only half accounted for by any conscious desire such as that of simplifying and lyricizing his themes, possibly to suit the taste of the young queen. The best explanation, I feel, lies in the pale, distant, and unreal character of the world in which the heroines were moving. Dramatic irony was not avoided; it was simply neglected.[17]

Much the same could be repeated in connection with the *Manciple's Tale.* The Ovidian apologue certainly offered one good suggestion of

[11] In the very scenes of *Philomela* which Chaucer weakens by suppressing ironical contrasts, he occasionally adds details, e.g., the distribution of presents (ll. 2303–4).

[12] Ll. 1978–84. [13] Ll. 2096–3000. [14] Ll. 2127 ff.

[15] *P.M.L.A.,* XX (1905), 802–18.

[16] In no other legend do I find Chaucer consciously adding dramatic irony. In line 2278, we have only a conventional and much weakened formula. Lines 855–61 slightly enlarge upon *Metamorphoses,* IV, 128, but Chaucer is only putting a little extra stress on the loveliness of his heroine, and, if Fate seems the more cruel for it, this is a purely accidental result.

[17] The same remarks apply to *Anelida and Arcite.* The narrative is unfinished, but even in the existing fragment, dramatic irony could have been used had Chaucer so desired.

dramatic irony—the raven's expectation of a reward[18]—plus an obvious opportunity for such irony: Phoebus' revulsion of feeling immediately after he has killed Coronis. Neither appears to have attracted Chaucer's attention. More puzzling is the presence in the *Manciple's Tale* of an ironical feature not paralleled in Ovid: Phoebus himself teaches a caged bird how to sing, with what results for the god's happiness the reader will recall. If Chaucer was not to bring out the dramatic irony of this motif, one cannot help wondering why he changed the Ovidian legend at this point; why the Olympian god, to whom birds freely used to fly, should be made to keep a bird in a cage. This, I believe, is one of several indications that Chaucer must have known some tell-tale-bird story of the fabliau type.[19] He tried to draw from both that source and the *Metamorphoses,* but was not entirely successful in fusing the elements together or in grasping the story as a whole. Without such grasp no dramatic irony was possible; indeed, no ironic contrast could even suggest itself to the poet's mind.[20]

## The "Monk's Tale"

By definition, every one of the Monk's "tragedies" is a wonderful chance for developing the irony of Fate:

> Tragedie is to seyn a certeyn storie, . . . .
> Of him that stood in greet prosperitee
> And is y-fallen out of heigh degree
> Into miserie, and endeth wrecchedly.[21]

And yet, we read the whole tale without really hoping to find any striking or beautiful stroke of dramatic irony: from the very beginning we feel that Chaucer's aim is to accumulate illustrations of the mutability of Fortune; that his interest is in this abstract theme rather than in his heroes. Besides, each account is too short[22] to leave sufficient room for the preparation of the irony of action.

[18] *Metamorphoses,* II, 534–632, reprinted in *Or. and An.,* pp. 439–40.

[19] A story of a husband who would keep a bird as a reporter on his wife's conduct (as is the case in all analogues mentioned by Clouston, except for Ovid, Chaucer, and Gower). Similarly, Phoebus' belief in the innocence of his wife, a belief so sudden and so entirely unaccounted for, strikes one as a recollection of a more logical story, possibly that alluded to by the Wife of Bath (D . 231–34) where a *"wys* wif" managed to look innocent. (This may have been a version close to that of the *Seven Wise Men,* where the husband, however, finally clears the case.)

[20] The *Mcp. T.* was probably written before Chaucer's appreciation of dramatic irony was fully developed.

[21] B . 3163–67. "Tragedie" is defined again in B . 3181–88, 3951–56.

[22] In Chaucer's sources as well as in the *Mk. T.*

## THE "CANON'S YEOMAN'S TALE"

The whole speech of the disappointed, embittered Yeoman was conceived by Chaucer as one violent outburst of resentment against alchemy and the alchemists. Careful, cold-blooded calculation of ironical effects would have been out of place in any part of that outburst. Besides, since the story told by the Yeoman was to be a denunciation of the "infinit falsenesse" of alchemists, the victim in the tale had to have all our sympathy and could not be ridiculed. Still, a deception plot had to be built—Chaucer probably derived it from his own acquaintance with the pretended science—and the temptation was strong to make the dupe, in typically fabliau fashion, spontaneously come halfway to meet his deceiver. To a very limited extent Chaucer seems to have yielded. There may not be any dramatic irony in the priest's readiness to accept the canon's suggestion[23] and to obey his every order,[24] for these reactions are hardly more than what we expected. But the praise of the canon's honesty in G. 1036–41 goes far beyond what we would have anticipated for such a natural gesture as the repayment of borrowed money. Similarly, the admiration and enthusiasm of the honest priest when the canon produces his plates of silver pass our expectations.[25] And certainly there is an ironical intention when the business propositions emanate, not from the deceiver, but from the future dupe.[26] A little more of this dramatic irony, and the emphasis would inevitably have been shifted from the deceitfulness of the canon to the priest's covetousness and gullibility. As a warning against the alchemists the tale would have been less convincing; as an expression of the Yeoman's feelings it would have been more seriously spoiled.

## THE "KNIGHT'S TALE"

Though there is dramatic irony in the *Knight's Tale,* the striking fact—the many turns of Fortune essential to the plot being kept in mind—is that the instances of dramatic irony should be so few. We can at once discard from our consideration all those opportunities furnished by incognitoes, chance meetings, soliloquies overheard, and other cheap, easy devices;[27] they were necessary to the development of the plot, but we must praise both Chaucer and his master Boccaccio for having felt that their rôle

[23] G. 1061–62.

[24] G. 1140–46, 1156–57, 1179–80, 1188, 1205–20, 1240–42, 1258–61.

[25] G. 1243–48, 1288–89, 1341–58.

[26] G. 1243–48, 1351 ff.

[27] E.g., the situation of Arcite as servant or squire at the court of Theseus; his soliloquy in the wood; the appearance of the heroine just when her two lovers are fighting for her; the account of the death of Emilia's fiancé (this last in the Italian only, *Tes.,* Bk. IV, st. 35).

should stop there. The subject offered many better chances for dramatic irony. In fact, the *Teseide* is full of ironical contrasts that even a hasty reader cannot fail to notice. First of all, they are set against the very favorable background of impressive Greek Fate.[28] Secondly, though Boccaccio never actually interrupts the story by stepping in himself to comment on the irony of life in the *Filostrato* manner, his deliberate calculation of effects often comes rather close to the surface. To give a few examples, when Arcita, owing to the friendly efforts of Peritoo, is set at liberty but at the same time banished from Athens, Boccaccio brings in a long dialogue between the two friends,[29] the only purpose of which is to emphasize the irony of the well-intentioned gesture. Later, when the heroine laments over Arcita's fate, her own consciousness of dramatic irony—a motif very beautiful in itself—is called upon to help ours.[30] In other cases, a quicker notation secures the effect;[31] in others, still, the reader may be left to notice the incongruity for himself—but then that incongruity is obvious enough: the two heroes' tender farewell in the prison[32] makes us think of their next meeting; at that next meeting (and later too), as Palemone proves no very lucky fighter, we smile, remembering that it was he who stubbornly insisted on fighting.[33]

Why did not Chaucer seize upon these and similar suggestions of Boccaccio as eagerly as he did when writing the *Troilus?* That he might have overlooked the chances for dramatic irony is out of the question, and condensation of the Italian epic would account for not more than a few sacrifices.[34] Neither is the philosophical background of Chaucer's poem less favorable than that of the *Teseide*.[35] Perhaps the suggestion of an

---

[28] On dramatic irony and determinism, see above, p. 10. [29] *Tes.*, Bk. III, st. 61–68.

[30] *Tes.*, Bk. X, st. 75:

> Ohimè che i fiori, i quanti allor coglieva,
> E'l canto, anzi fu pianto, ch'io cantava
> Erinni, o lassa, tutto ciò moveva.

(“*Erinni*” is often singular in Old Italian; we can accept it here as subject of “*moveva.*”)

[31] E.g., *ibid.*, Bk. IV, st. 24, ll. 1–2 (cf. A . 1553–54) ; Bk. IX, st. 8, l. 1.

[32] *Ibid.*, Bk. III, st. 74–81. [33] *Ibid.*, Bk. V, st. 38 ff.

[34] E.g., *ibid.*, Bk. I, st. 116–17, the whole Amazone episode being suppressed in the *Kn. T.*

[35] Though it is less lofty and imposing: the gods have “swich strif” about the issue! Also, less emphasis is laid on the former tragedies of the Theban royal house, to which the Greek Fate of the *Tes.* owed much of its grandeur (*Tes.*, Bk. V, st. 57–59). On the other hand, determinism in the hands of Chaucer is made more acceptable to fourteenth-century readers by the identification of pagan gods and planets, by references to dates accepted as lucky or unlucky (A . 1462–63, 1850), and by the Boethian coloring of the soliloquies on predestination (A . 1251–72, 1303–24). See Walter C. Curry, *Chaucer and the Mediaeval Sciences* (New York, 1926), pp. 149–63.

answer is offered by Professor J. Hulbert's interesting paper "What Was Chaucer's Aim in the *Knight's Tale?*"[36] Mr. Hulbert's thesis is that "Chaucer saw in the *Teseide* a plot which, with some alterations, could be used effectively to present one of these problems of love which the votaries of courtly love enjoyed considering . . . .: 'which of the two young men, of equal worth and with almost equal claims, shall (or should) win the lady?' " It will be Palamon, because he has the sense to appeal to Venus rather than to Mars. The merit of this theory is that it offers an explanation—to my mind the first acceptable explanation—of Chaucer's simplification of the three main characters as found in the *Teseide*. The Italian Arcita and Palemone were very distinct persons; but Chaucer could not allow any particular feature of either of his two heroes, any individuality of Emilia, or any preference of hers, to interfere with the reader's rational consideration of a question of courtly love.

The bearing of this on our subject is clear: since many of Chaucer's finest and strongest instances of dramatic irony depend for their effectiveness on good characterization, material from which such characterization was excluded could hardly encourage our poet to emphasize the dramatic irony inherent in the plot—e.g., the irony of Arcite's victory—or to add many new contrasts in the hope of achieving ironical effects. Only a few such contrasts are created with what appears to be an ironical intention. Thus, it is Arcite, soon to be released, who expresses his resignation to live and die in prison.[37] Set at liberty, he reflects on the good luck of Palamon, while the latter in turn envies his rival for his new opportunities.[38] In the same soliloquies the two heroes discuss predestination. To quote Mr. Jefferson, "more pity is aroused for Arcite, that he who acknowledges that God's ways are always just meets in the moment of his greatest triumph a sudden and tragic death, whereas Palamon who complains against heaven receives the high reward."[39] But the two heroes are, on the whole, too much alike for any irony resulting from their different attitudes in one particular scene[40] to be noticed on first or even second reading.

---

[36] *University of North Carolina Studies in Philology,* XXVI (1929), 375–85. See also P. F. Baum, "Characterization in the *Knight's Tale,*" *Mod. Lang. Notes,* XLVI (1931), 302–4.

[37] A . 1084–91.

[38] A . 1234–43 and 1281–94. In Boccaccio, Palemone is jealously suspicious of Arcita (Bk. IV, st. 60; Bk. V, st. 2, 9), but nothing is said of Arcita's envy of Palemone's fate.

[39] B. Jefferson, *Chaucer and the "Consolation of Philosophy" of Boethius,* p. 131.

[40] In another scene (A . 1542 ff.), Arcite complains against the cruelty and injustice of the Olympian gods.

Some particular touches of dramatic irony present in the *Teseide* would not only be weakened in the *Knight's Tale* as understood by Dr. Hulbert but would become impossible. Since the heroes are to be rivals from the first—the problem of courtly love rests on this rivalry—the irony of their tender farewell in the prison must be sacrificed; if our sympathy must be equally divided between the two lovers, Palemone's mad insistence on a fight must also be suppressed; if Emelye is to be a mere name, one graceful touch of delicately ironical comedy is lost, viz., the little mistake of the Italian Arcita deploring a situation in which

> Per giovinezza l'Emilia non sente
> Che cosa sia ancora innamorare.[41]

By some accident, however, this same simplification of Emilia's character opens an opportunity for another ironic situation which the English Theseus interprets for us in familiar Pandarus fashion.[42] The two heroes have been fighting for Emelye:

> But this is yet the beste game of alle,
> That she, for whom they han this Iolitee,
> Can hem ther-for as muche thank as me;
> She woot namore of al this hote fare,
> By God, than woot a cokkow or an hare![43]

We enjoy the passage because the irony is real and amusing enough, and also—shall we confess it?—because the truly human smile of good Theseus brings in a most welcome change of atmosphere. In the *Teseide,* where Emilia more than suspects her two lovers' feelings, a similar remark would have been a joke on the speaker himself, i.e., an entirely different ironic implication, and one of course unthinkable in Boccaccio's epic. For the lines quoted above, the nearest to a hint in the Italian poem would be Arcita's remark about the absurdity of a fight:

> "combatteremo
> E colle spade in man farem le parti
> Di quella cosa la qual non avemo."[44]

To sum up, led by the central idea of his tale to reduce to the barest possible outlines the main characters of Boccaccio's *Teseide,* Chaucer felt that little could be gained by exposing three rather conventional figures to

---

[41] *Tes.,* Bk. IV, st. 76. See also Bk. IV, st. 82, l. 8, and st. 86, ll. 1–2, and compare with Bk. III, st. 18–19 and Bk. IV, st. 57–58.

[42] The fact that Theseus keeps his individuality in the *Kn. T.* seems to support Professor Hulbert's view: simplification of characters was a sacrifice for Chaucer, and he did not carry it any farther than was required by the *Kn. T.* as he had conceived it.

[43] A. 1806–10.

[44] *Tes.,* Bk. V, st. 52.

even the subtlest tricks of Fortune. He accordingly made very few attempts in that direction; from beginning to end, his interest was elsewhere.

### The "Clerk's Tale"

To a plot built of such unexpected turns as that of the *Clerk's Tale,* it would be only too easy to add the piquancy of successive strokes of dramatic irony by contrasting, for instance, Griselda's sorrow and resignation with the happy issue, or the courtiers' comments with the real intentions of the marquis. This would be easy enough; but could these touches be really effective in surroundings as unreal as those of the *Clerk's Tale?* For the inconceivable is everywhere, in the characters as in the intrigue.[45] We feel too far from our world of human beings to wonder at any possible incongruity or feel the slightest temptation to raise questions. Like his masters Boccaccio and Petrarch, Chaucer saw that the promises of the subject were elsewhere—in the lovely figure of patient Griselda—and wisely abstained from trying to reach dramatic effects through the irony of circumstances.

### The Three Pious Legends

In none of the tales of the *Man of Law,* the *Prioress,* and the *Second Nun,* do we find any dramatic irony at all. Could this be due to a momentary inertness of Chaucer's inventive powers? A much better explanation is offered by some characteristics essential to the genre to which the three stories belong. Different as they are in other respects, and no matter what their ultimate origin may be,[46] all three are treated by Chaucer in the spirit of pious legends. Not only are they drawn on a background of Christian faith—most of the stories told by medieval writers are—but they are almost one with that background; their idealism detaches them from earth and transfers them to a higher sphere very close to heaven and to the overruling power of Providence. That power is more than an

[45] Chaucer has only one touch of dramatic irony, a pleasant and natural one, but it occurs before the story takes its too unreal turn; I mean Griselda's naïve curiosity about the new marquise. Interestingly enough, both Petrarch and Chaucer have left records of their appreciation of this charming little touch, Petrarch having given the point more stress than Boccaccio, and Chaucer more than Petrarch. With E. 274–87 (the direct discourse of E. 281–87 is not paralleled in the Italian or Latin) compare Petrarch ("*Griseldis omnium quae erga se pararentur ignara, peractis quae agenda domi erant, aquam et longinquo fonte convectans, paternum limen intrabat, ut expedita curis aliis, ad visendam Domini sui sponsam cum puellis comitibus properaret*") and Boccaccio ("*e giunti a casa del padre della fanciulla, e lei trovata, che con acqua tornava della fonte in gran fretta, per andar con altre femmine a veder venire la sposa di Gualtieri*").

[46] In origin, the *M.L.T.* is probably a fairy story.

object of firm faith; it is a reality, a close and immediate reality, not only for the author but for the reader, whatever his personal beliefs may be.

The very definiteness of such a background greatly limits the effectiveness of possible irony of action. For really striking dramatic irony always involves an element of uneasy intellectual surprise at those mysterious forces that seem to take pleasure in creating incongruities in our lives. But such definiteness can only weaken dramatic irony. There is a further factor that makes the use of the device almost unthinkable in the three tales under consideration: the Christian Providence back of the legends of saints is a power too simple in its goodness to take any pleasure in weaving absurdities. It is concerned only with the triumph of the good and the punishment of the wicked—two most sharply distinct classes—and toward both ends it works in perfectly straight lines. The good are taken as if by the hand through a sequence of trials planned as steps for their steady ascent. The wicked, alas, have to be brought into the picture, not so much as foils but as persecutors, i.e., as indispensable agents in the saints' progress toward heaven. When divine vengeance overtakes them, it kills them with one blow, leaving no chance for any ups and downs in their fortunes. And this brings us to one more reason why the ironies of Fate would be out of place in the typical pious legend: its object is not to record events but to glorify the virtues of a saint; it is much more lyric and rhetorical than narrative. We are taken to a world where everything appears harmonious and simple. If the irony of human actions brought us back to the frets, and tensions, and incongruities of this world, sharp angles would destroy the beautiful and regular curve: the golden thread would be broken.[47]

Whether Chaucer ever reflected on the discordant note which dramatic irony would strike in a pious legend, I shall not attempt to decide.[48] But certain it is that, either by instinct or by reflection, he was safely and consistently guarded against the danger of using it.

His abstention, in the case of the *Second Nun's Tale,* is not very surprising; the account of St. Cecilia's life in Jacobus de Voragine offered no specially inviting opportunity. In the *Prioress' Tale* it would have been easy enough to bring out the irony of little Hugh's happy song, of the Jews' plans, of the mother's search for her already dead boy, etc. But

[47] To a lesser extent, these remarks apply to the *Physician's Tale.* Chaucer here freely enlarges on his source (his tale is four times as long as the account in the *Roman de la Rose,* ll. 5843 ff.) but, as he wishes to shift the emphasis from the injustice of Appius to the charm and spotless purity of Virginia, he almost completely avoids dramatic irony. See only, in C. 146–48, the judge's premature exultation.

[48] His choice of meter is interesting in this connection; it shows that he was clearly aware of the primarily lyrical character that the tales were to take.

Chaucer resisted every one of these temptations. He went farther in the *Man of Law's Tale,* consistently suppressing whatever looked like dramatic irony in his source, Trivet's *Life of Constance.*[49] Three passages are worth noting: (*a*) In Trivet, the Roman senator Arsenius, to whom Constance has been brought, fails to recognize her, and not only tells her about her own life but about her death![50] Chaucer has to keep the same marvelous meeting, but all contrasts not strictly necessary are suppressed. (*b*) When King Alle, the husband of Constance, arrives in Rome, Trivet lodges him in the castle of Arsenius, in which Constance is living. Unaware of any relation between Alle and Constance, Arsenius announces the visitor, upon which Constance swoons for joy.[51] Chaucer, of course, has to keep the meeting of Arsenius and King Alle, but all the rest is omitted. (*c*) When the Roman emperor is asked to come to that dinner at which he does not suspect that he will meet his lost daughter Constance, Trivet makes him first answer that he is still mourning the death of his daughter, and accordingly cannot go, but a minute later accept the invitation because entreated *"pur lamur qil auoit al alme sa fille Constaunce."*[52] In the *Man of Law's Tale* the emperor grants the request immediately. In short, Chaucer leaves out all the contrasts not strictly indispensable for the progress of the action. In a glorification of Providence, in the life of a saint that was not to be humanized at all, the poet was careful to avoid what would have shifted the emphasis from the mood to the details and intricacies of the plot.

Chaucer's abstention from dramatic irony in the three pious legends is one of many illustrations of his keen power of distinguishing among literary genres. At the same time it affords one of our best proofs of the perfect awareness with which our poet used the device in other works.

[49] *Or. and An.,* pp. 1–53. Chaucer's condensation of that source is no sufficient explanation. Gower, whose version is considerably shorter than the *M.L.T.,* keeps most of the dramatic situations found in Trivet (*Confessio Amantis,* ed. Pauli, I, 179–213).

[50] Gower passes more lightly over this episode, but he keeps some of the irony of Trivet's account (*op. cit.,* p. 199).

[51] In Gower (p. 204), King Alle is not to be lodged in the castle of Arsenius, but the episode of the swooning is kept much the same.

[52] The corresponding passage in Gower is substantially the same.

# X. CONCLUSIONS

In the course of our study we have noted different literary influences at work in the growth and education of Chaucer's sense of dramatic irony. Let us now combine our observations. Two main influences stand out—*Il Filostrato* and the fabliaux. In addition, there are several literary genres—the *exemplum* literature, the animal epic, the folk tales—each of which supplied one plot involving irony of action; but no deep or lasting effect of any of those genres is noticeable.

Let us take Chaucer at the beginning of his productive life. In his first choice of masters lies a partial explanation of the total absence of dramatic irony in the works that preceded the *Troilus.* The French literature imitated in the allegorical poems had no place for the irony of action (even the *Roman de la Rose* offered nothing but the conventional phraseology on Fortune); and, in the Latin classics, the dramatic contrasts were generally presented in a harsh rhetorical fashion that as a rule failed to draw Chaucer's attention. Still, we have noticed that, even in his early allegories, he revealed uncommon dramatic sense. Let any good teacher come, and the young poet's latent taste for dramatic irony will easily be stirred to action.

The good teacher came, and in most favorable circumstances. For he came offering a poem, *Il Filostrato,* which Chaucer determined to study thoroughly and to use, not in parts as he did the *Roman de la Rose* or the *Filocolo,* but in its entirety; hence he acquired a perfect grasp of the whole narrative and a full appreciation of ironical contrasts, both tragic and humorous, which in fact it was impossible not to see. For Boccaccio had rarely contented himself with giving merely the elements of those contrasts. More frequently he had inserted a parenthesis to tell his readers: Here lies a contrast; we must stop for a moment; here is Troilus, glorying in his freedom, and there is the god of love preparing to strike him. Do you see the irony now? Chaucer did see it, and he saw many more such contrasts, some vaguely indicated in the *Filostrato* and others that Boccaccio had not even suggested. As he had no objection to enlarging upon his Italian model, nothing restricted the freedom with which he indulged the newly acquired taste. Perhaps, in this sudden awakening, recollections of other readings were brought up: Latin classics? Dante? some fabliaux? We have one indication of a recollection of Juvenal in connection with an ironical situation indicated in *Troilus and Criseyde,* not in the *Filostrato,*[1]

[1] *Tr. and Cr.,* IV, 197 ff.

but we have nothing else. And certainly, Chaucer's spontaneous acceptance of the technique of Boccaccio in some original parts of the *Troilus* strongly speaks in favor of what I think is the very direct and unrivaled influence of the *Filostrato* at that period. The rest of Boccaccio's works can be almost disregarded here. Chaucer occasionally drew upon the other early narratives of the Italian master,[2] but none of them (not even the *Teseide*) was the object of the same thorough and meticulous study as the *Filostrato*. As to the *Decameron,* it does not seem either to have suggested to our poet any particular ironical situation, or to have influenced his handling of such motifs taken from other sources. This total lack of any indication of indebtedness in the use of a device so frequently resorted to by both writers certainly supports the view that Chaucer knew little, if anything, of Boccaccio's masterpiece.

Before the opening of the Canterbury period, Chaucer had thus acquired a full appreciation of the resources of dramatic irony, both for humor and for pathos; he had shown himself eager to take those resources into account, but in one poem only—never before, and, more important, not afterward. For at least some of the *Legend of Good Women* must have been written after the *Troilus,*[3] and we have seen that Chaucer neglected there excellent opportunities for tragic irony. Roughly—very roughly—about 1387, the question is thus pending whether our poet will use the device any more, whether he will not forsake, together with the fatalistic background of the *Troilus,* his sense of the incongruities formerly connected, to a large extent, with that background.

He will, in fact, keep up his interest in dramatic irony, and develop a greater skill in presenting it. Here the influence of the French fabliaux comes in. They were full of the irony of circumstances, especially of dupes running into snares often laid with their own hands. What a feast for the writer of *Troilus and Criseyde!* To say that his liking for dramatic irony determined his choice among the fabliaux would be to exaggerate, for he needed good stories, and this need implies more than one type of requirement. But certainly he wanted humorous situations, and nothing creates them more surely than the irony of action. Though demonstration is out of the question, one feels certain that such irony was relatively more frequent in the sources of Chaucer's fabliaux—of the *Reeve's,* the *Miller's,*

---

[2] When the *Filocolo* half dictated the main dramatic motif of the *Fkl. T.,* Chaucer's skill in handling dramatic irony was already at its highest.

[3] Very shortly after its completion (which makes the absence of dramatic irony the more interesting) if Professor Root is right in seeing in *Tr. and Cr.,* III, 624–28, an allusion to an astronomical event of May 1385 (R. K. Root and H. N. Russell, "A Planetary Date for Chaucer's *Troilus,*" *P.M.L.A.,* XXXIX [1924], 48–63).

and the *Shipman's Tales*—than in the total of the fabliau literature known to him (of which total the *Recueil* of Montaiglon probably gives us a fair idea). As to the way in which Chaucer added incongruous situations to incongruous situations, and still more remarkably exploited the material of his predecessors by supplementing their hurried accounts with his own excellent character drawing, I can only refer to chapter iii of this study. But I wish to draw attention once more to the lesson that the trouvères imparted to Chaucer with regard to technique, the lesson of consistent objectivity, of quickness and lightness of touch so different from the method of comment and disclosure of the "ficelles" repeatedly noted in the *Troilus*. In the French trouvères this was mostly natural, unsophisticated directness; in Chaucer, who had abandoned Boccaccio's technique for theirs, it cannot be anything but conscious skill in the concealment of skill. The change in our poet's method was for the better. And yet the value and opportuneness of Boccaccio's teaching could hardly be overestimated. Had not the *Filostrato* come first, the contrasts lightly indicated by the French trouvères would probably not have been appreciated by our poet as susceptible of the same interesting developments.

To these two main influences of the *Filostrato* and the fabliaux, possibly a third should be added, that of the Breton tales. Chaucer's excellent imitation of a lay in the *Franklin's Tale* reveals thorough familiarity with the genre, and it may be worth remembering here that the main change brought by our poet to the Italian source of his "Breton" lay creates an ironical touch superior to, but belonging to the same class as, the intense and deeply pathetic irony of *Les dous amanz*. How far the influence may have extended, it is impossible to say.

To Chaucer's natural gifts and to his training mainly at the hands of Boccaccio and the trouvères, we are indebted for those many beautiful strokes of dramatic irony that have been analyzed in the course of this study. Should we now try to condense our results and characterize in one line Chaucer's use of dramatic irony, I would suggest the four words: deliberateness; variety; creativeness; and sincerity.

Of Chaucer's deliberate calculation of the effects of dramatic irony, no very strong proof should be required, for the better we know our poet, the less "naïve" he appears. We have, however, plenty of proofs: the number of the instances (compare, in this respect, the *Canterbury Tales* to Gower's *Confessio Amantis*); the sureness of Chaucer's feeling as to where and when dramatic irony should be avoided; his early technique of telling us that there *is* a contrast; and, finally, his even more significant later technique of partly subordinating to the possibilities of dramatic irony this most Chaucerian of all features, the delineation of character.

Variety is the trait that will strike us first if we compare Chaucer's narratives to—let us take an extreme case—the works of Thomas Hardy. True it is that the gloomy, awe-inspiring mood created by the tragic ironies of Hardy's novels finds no exact parallel in Chaucer. But what a beautifully wide range of effects we are offered instead—pure humor in Simkin's short triumph, intense tragic effect in the revelers' quest of Death, harsh satire in the *Merchant's Tale,* genial optimism in the scene of Antigone's song! And, besides such examples, characterized by a comparatively definite mood, we find all the subtle scale of delicate and complex nuances, of humor in tragedy, of emotion in laughter—

Chaucer's creativeness in the field of dramatic irony has been noted again and again. His treatment of ironical contrasts supplied by his sources can, to a very large extent, be called creative on account of the new intensity and interest imparted to nearly every one of those motifs by the subtleties of Chaucer's presentation. But many of our poet's best strokes of dramatic irony—those of the *Wife's Prologue,* of the largest portion of the *Merchant's Tale,* of the rock motif in the *Franklin's Tale*—find no parallel at all in any antecedent. They owe their existence to the poet's perception of the ironical coloring which details, void of any such connotation in their first setting, could acquire when woven into the fabric of his own narratives. This, I believe, is as far as inventiveness can go within the field that we have been studying.

Finally, by Chaucer's sincerity in the presentation of the irony of action, I mean his conception of those little absurdities as part of his life and ours. Had dramatic irony appealed to him simply as a trick of narrative art, he would naturally have had recourse to it when his subject interested him least. Exactly the opposite occurs. Because Ovid's world seems so unreal, the irony of action has no meaning there; because the Good Women of the *Legend* are rather pale figures in Chaucer's mind, he fails to be moved by the very real incongruities of their lives. But let us turn to the best and most realistic portions of Chaucer's works, and we find that humorous or tragic irony of action almost naturally takes its place in the very lives of Simkin and January, the Wife of Bath, Troilus and Criseyde.[4] Significantly enough, Troilus and Criseyde are at the same time Chaucer's first great success in character drawing and his first real opportunity for feeling and conveying impressions of dramatic irony. In another respect they deserve our attention here: in Boccaccio's epic, Troilo was the only actor who perceived the irony of his past actions. In *Troilus and Criseyde,* Pandarus

[4] This conception of dramatic irony accounts for the limits set to Chaucer's use of the device. The fabliaux offered him enough examples of dramatic irony built on incognitoes, puns, concealment, prolonged conversations at cross purposes, etc. Through all these temptations, Chaucer maintained his high standard of realism.

and even Criseyde are credited with the same sense.[5] Other heroes of Chaucer's will follow, all carefully chosen among those characters who otherwise reveal a reflective turn of mind: Theseus, the Justinus of the *Merchant's Tale,* Aleyn and John the clerks. The different passages in which we see them smile or grin at incongruities in the world around them help in creating a feeling that dramatic irony, far from being the conscious projection of the poet's mind into his subject, belongs to that very subject as the great humorist could not choose but see it; that literary influences only helped him to interpret in his own work what was in fact an essential element of his view of life in its tragic and comic aspects.

[5] A very clear sense in the case of Pandarus; a rather vague one in that of Criseyde. See *Tr. and Cr.,* IV, 827–33; V, 1054–57.

# INDEX


## A

*Anelida and Arcite,* 85 n.
Astrology and fatalism, in *Tr. and Cr.,* 13; in *Kn. T.,* 88 n.

## B

BOCCACCIO, GIOVANNI, summary of influence on Chaucer, 94–95, 96; *see also* Dramatic irony, *and under* separate works
Breton lays, dramatic irony in, 67 n.; possible influence on Chaucer, 96

## C

*Canterbury Tales, see* Frame of *C.T., and under* separate tales
Characterization, *see* Dramatic irony, *and under* separate works
CHAUCER, GEOFFREY, progress in dramatic irony, 94–96; main influences, 94–96; characters of dramatic irony, 96–98; *see also under* separate works
Classics, fatalism in *Tr. and Cr.,* 11; rhetorical irony without influence on Chaucer, 83–86, 94; *see also under* separate works
*Cook's Tale,* 9

## D

*Decameron,* example of dramatic irony in, 8; analogues to *C.T.,* 32 n., 39 n., 41, 54 n., 62 n., 63 n.; prolonged unnatural situations in, 33; typical introduction to irony, 34
Dramatic irony
  Anticipations of dénouement, in *Fil.* and *Tr. and Cr.,* 11–12, 14 n.; in *Reeve's Prologue,* 28; in French fabliaux, 28, 31, 36; in *Mil. T.,* 36
  Characterization, creating or accentuating irony, in *Tr. and Cr.,* 13, 17–18, 19, 21–23, 24, 26; in *Rv. T.,* 28–29, 34, 35; in source of *Rv. T.,* 31–35; creating subtle irony, in *Rv. T.,* 34; in *Sh. T.,* 40; in *Mil. T., Sh. T.,* and *Mch. T.,* compared to fabliaux, 36, 37–38, 39, 42, 55, 57; in *Fkl. T.,* compared to *Filocolo,* 63; in *N.P.T.,* compared to source, 69–71; satiric, in *Sum. T.,* 45; conventional, *see* Fabliaux; absence of, *see Kn. T.*
  Comments on, in *Fil.,* 14–16, 94–95, 96; imitated in *Tr. and Cr.,* 15–16, 19–20, 25; in *Decam.,* 34, 63 n.; in classics, 46, 83, 84 n., 85, 94
  Concentration on one contrast in *Pd. T.,* 77
  Cruelty in, in *Tr. and Cr.,* 23; in *Sh. T.,* 40, 42; in *Mch. T.,* 52–53, 54; compared to source, 56–57
  Definition and examples, 7–9
  Humor in, in *Tr. and Cr.,* 16; in *Rv. T.,* 28, 29, 34, 35; with pathos, in *Mil. T.,* 37–38; in *W.B.P.,* 81; with cruelty, in *Sh. T.,* 40, 41–42; in *Kn. T.,* 90
  Indefinite contrasts creating, *see Mch. T.*
  Mood preparing for, in *Pd. T.,* 77
  Neglect of, in *Legend,* 83–85; in *Mcp. T.,* 85–86
  Objective presentation of, in *Tr. and Cr.,* 20–21, 24, 26; in French fabliaux, 34–35, 45, 96; in Chaucer's fabliaux and later works, 35; in *Fkl. T.,* 65; in *Pd. T.,* 78; in *W.B.P.,* 81
  Pathos, in *Mil. T.,* 37–38; in *Fkl. T.,* 65; in *W.B.P.,* 81
  Perception of, by the characters, in *Tr. and Cr.,* 17; in *Rv. T.,* 30; in *Mch. T.,* 52–53; in *Kn. T.,* 90; as indication of Chaucer's sincerity, 97–98
  Philosophical background, of fatalism, in *Tr. and Cr.,* 10–13; in *Fil.,* 10–12; in classics, 11; in *N.P.T.,* 71; in *Pd. T.,* 78–79; in *Mk. T.,* 86; in *Kn. T.,* 88; of Christian faith, in *Pd. T.,* 79; in pious legends, 91–92; definiteness of background, 8; in *Tr. and Cr.,* 13; in *Pd. T.,* 79; in pious legends, 92

Dramatic irony (*Continued*)
Poetic justice, 9 n.; in fabliaux, 34–35, 35 n.; in *Pd. T.*, 79; in pious legends, 92
Sacrifice of, in *Tr. and Cr.*, 18–19; in *Sum. T.*, 46; in *Pd. T.*, 77; in *C.Y.T.*, 87; in *Kn. T.*, 88–91; in *Cl. T.*, 91; in pious legends, 91–93; as indication of Chaucer's deliberateness, 96
Satire, in *Fr. T.*, 42, 45; in *Sum. T.*, 45–46
Tragic feeling, in *Tr. and Cr.*, 17; in *W.B.P.*, 81
*Duchess, Book of the,* Fortune in, 10; dramatic situation in, 14 n.

F

Fabliaux, in *C.T.*, on sources, 27; French fabliaux, irony of situations in, 28, 33 n., 35–36, 38, 47, 95–96; introductions, 28, 36; conventional characterization, 31, 36, 37–38, 39, 41 n.; poetic justice in, 34–35; objective presentation of irony, 35; cruelty, 37–38; Chaucer's debt to, 35, 95–96; *see also under* separate works
Frame of *C.T.*, irony explained by, in *Sh. T.*, 42; in *Fr. T.*, 44–45; in *Sum. T.*, 45–46; one irony suggested by, in *Mch. T.*, 52–53; the Host's mistakes, 80; Professor Tupper's ironical tales, 80 n.; lives of Host and Reeve, 80; of Wife of Bath, 80–81; dramatic irony in independent realistic work, 81–82
*Franklin's Tale,* source of, in the *Filocolo,* 62; dramatic irony in tale and source, 62–64; characterization, 63–65; the rock task, 64; reticence, 65; quality of irony, 65; Professor Tatlock on source of rock motif, 65–66; Celtic background, 66 n.; irony in Breton lays, 66, 67 n., 96
*Friar's Tale,* attack upon Summoner, 42, 44–45; realism sacrificed to satire, 42–45; four motifs, 42–45; irony in source, 44

G

Gower, John, 59, 60 n., 93 n., 96

H

Hardy, Thomas, 8, 65 n., 97
*Hous of Fame,* dramatic situation in, 14 n.
Hulbert, Professor J., on Chaucer's aim in *Kn. T.*, 89–90

K

*Knight's Tale,* opportunities in situations, 87; cases of irony in *Tes.*, 88; Fate in *Tes.* and *Kn. T.*, 88; Professor Hulbert's theory and absence of irony, 89–90; the rivals' fight, 90

L

La Fontaine, analogues to *C.T.*, 32 n., 39 n., 54 n.
*Legend of Good Women,* dramatic irony neglected, 83–84, 84 n.; irony in *Ariadne,* 85; *Legend* contrasted to realistic works, 97
Lowes, Professor J. L., on *Le Miroir de Mariage,* 47 n., 49 n.; on *Tes.* and *Ariadne,* 85

M

*Man of Law's Tale,* dramatic irony of Trivet avoided, 93
Manly, Professor J. M., on lucky days in *Tr. and Cr.*, 13 n.
Melibeus, 9, 48 n., 53
Merchant, the, allusion to, in *Sh. T.*, 42; his blow at Wife of Bath, 50; *see also Merchant's Tale*
*Merchant's Tale,* place in marriage group, 46; use of irony suggested by fabliaux and *Miroir,* 46–48; summary of *Miroir,* 47; debts to *Miroir,* 47, 49 n., 54 n., 55 n.; sustained bitterness, 48, 57–58; age of January, 48; anticipations of dénouement, 48, 49 n.; fusion of pear tree story with *Miroir,* 49–50 n.; January's hopes, 48, 49 n., 51, 52–53; direct irony of Merchant, 49 n.; elusive contrasts (warm wax, trees), 51, 53; cruel irony, 52–53, 54, 56, 57; marriage ritual, 53–54; January's happiness, 54; source of pear tree story, 54 n.; parallels with *Mil. T.*, 55; echo of *Tr. and Cr.*, 55; last

scenes compared with *Novellino,* 56–57; pathos and tragedy in fabliau material, 57

*Miller's Tale,* ironical motifs in source, 35–36, 38; anticipation of dénouement in Prologue, 36; Chaucerian characterization, 36; parallels with *Mch. T.,* 37 n.; pathos with humor, 37–38; fabliau type of irony, 38

N

*Nun's Priest's Tale,* humor in animal epic, 68; deceiver deceived in *N.P.T.,* and analogues, 68–69; Chauntecleer's feeling of security, 69–70; the source, characterization in it, 70–71; Destiny, 71

O

Ovid, dramatic irony without influence on Chaucer, 83–85, 97

P

*Pardoner's Tale,* analogues to, 72; irony in Italian miracle, 72–73, 74; in Sachs's *Dot im Stock,* 73–74, 78; main source probably an *exemplum,* 74–75, 76 n.; concentration on one irony in *exemplum* quoted, 75–77; in *Pd. T.,* 77; atmosphere created in introduction, 77; the enigmatic old man, 77–78; brevity in dénouement, 78 n.; indefinite Christian background, 79

Patch, Howard R., on determinism in *Tr. and Cr.,* 12 n.

Petersen, Miss Kate O., on source of *N.P.T.,* 70 n., 71; on Thomas of Cantimpré and the *Pd. T.,* 74 n.

*Physician's Tale,* 92 n.

Pious legends, dramatic irony impossible in, 91–92; lyrical character of, 92; *see also under* separate tales

Poetic justice, *see* Dramatic irony

*Prioress' Tale,* 92–93

R

*Reeve's Tale,* the source, 27; introduction in Prologue, 28; characterization for the sake of irony, 28–29; Simkin's success, 29–30; his direct irony, 30–31; the clerks' perception of dramatic irony, 30; cradle episode, 32–33; irony of situation condensed from French fabliau, 33 n.; humor in cake episode, 34; Chaucer's brief summary, 34; objective presentation, 35; poetic justice, 34–35, 35 n.; Chaucer's debt to source and improvement on it, 35

*Roman de la Rose,* Fortune in, 13, 94; echoes of, in *W.B.P.,* 81; absence of dramatic irony in, 94

Root, Professor R. K., on Diomede's courtship, 21; on date of *Legend,* 95 n.

S

*Second Nun's Tale,* 92

Seneca, 46

*Shipman's Tale,* main irony in source, 39; characterization develops typical fabliau feature, 39; subtle irony, 40; cruelty, 40, 42; one irony in dénouement, 41; first attribution to Wife of Bath, 42

*Squire's Tale,* 9

*Summoner's Tale,* irony of situations in French analogue, 45; satiric characterization, 45–46; sermon against anger, 45; sacrifice of Seneca's irony, 46

T

Tatlock, Professor J. S. P., on *Tr. and Cr.* and *Mch. T.,* 55; on source of rock motif in *Fkl. T.,* 65–66

*Teseide,* as source of *Kn. T.,* 14 n., 87–90; setting of *Ariadne,* 85

*Thopas, Tale of Sir,* 9

*Troilus and Criseyde,* 10–26
- Antenor, 19–20
- Antigone, soothing delicate irony of her song, 24
- Astrology and fatalism, 13
- Benoît de Sainte-Maure, 18, 20, 23
- Boethius and determinism, 11, 88 n.
- Characterization creating or intensifying dramatic irony, 13, 17–18, 21–23
- Comedy created by Chaucer, 24, 26
- Comments of author on irony, in *Fil.,* 14–16; in *Tr. and Cr.,* 15–16, 19–20, 25

*Troilus and Criseyde* (*Continued*)
Criseyde, her love of fidelity, 13, 17–18, 21–23; the parting visit, 15; J. S. Craydon on her character, 17 n.; her care of her reputation, 18; her remorse, 18, 23; her first hesitations, 22, 24
Cruelty in dramatic irony, 23
Deiphebus, episode in his house, 24–25
Diomede, first mentions of his name, 18–19; his courtship, 21; Criseyde's fidelity to him, 23
Fatalism, as background for irony, 10; influence of Boccaccio, 10; of Boethius and Dante, 11–12; of the classics, 11; Troilus on predestination, 12; H. Patch about fatalism, 12 n.; the Trojan war, 12–13; astrology, lucky days, 13; Criseyde led by Fate, 13, 17–18, 24; indefiniteness of, 13; fatalism and main ironical motives, 14
*Filostrato, Il,* fatalistic background, 10; war setting, 13 n., 20; instances of dramatic irony, 14–19; irony pointed out, 14–16; characterization, 17; influence on Chaucer, 15, 19–20, 26, 94–95, 96
Humor in dramatic irony, 16
Objective presentation of dramatic irony, 20–21, 24, 26
Palladion feast, 15–17
Pandarus, his perception of dramatic irony, 17; his delight in irony, 25
Sacrifice of dramatic irony, 18–19
Tragedy in dramatic irony, 17, 23
Troilus, on fatalism, 12; his perception of dramatic irony, 17; faith in Criseyde, 21; jealousy, 21 n., 26; feigned illness, 25
War setting in, 12–13, 20, 24
TUPPER, PROFESSOR F., on sermons by sinners, 80 n.

V

VIRGIL, 84 n.

W

Wife of Bath, *Sh. T.* first attributed to her, 42; attacks of Merchant, 50; of Justinus, 52; *see also* Frame of *C.T.*
*Wife of Bath's Tale,* Middle English analogues, 59 ff.; crime of knight, 59 n.; dramatic irony in folk tales, 59–60, 60 n., 61; the knight's assurance, 60; unnamed boon motif, 60; transformation motif, 61